CHRONOLOGICAL
ATLAS OF
THE BIBLE

J. E. HOLLEY

THIRD MILLENNIUM PRESS LIMITED

DATING EVENTS IN THE BIBLE

The Bible itself contains no dates. Clerics and scholars over the centuries have attempted to date events – in particular the Creation, the Deluge and the Crucifixion of Jesus Christ within the historical context in the Roman world of emperors and governors. The Jewish calendar's complexity, with its ceremonies and records, adds to the confusion. Astronomical events calculations form a part of the variables, as do the systems of reckoning based on the Solar and Lunar cycles.

Dionysius Exiguus

Calendar calculations have to be adjusted for the Jewish, Julian and Gregorian Calendars. Dionysius Exiguus of Sythia Minor (Dennis the Small, AD470–544), having provided the system of *Anno Domini*, usually shortened to AD, for reckoning dates from the birth of Christ; and the *Anno Mundi* system (AM) based on dates from Creation. In fact, one earlier scholar maintained that AD1 was just eight days long (there having been, of course, no AD zero.)

Archbishop James Ussher (1581–1656), by working backwards, produced a Biblical chronology and fixed Creation as 23 October 4004BC. He researched widely amongst ancient sources, mastered the calendars of antiquity and reconciled a plethora of conflicting dates by reference to the Hebrew Bible. He fixed the Crucifixion at Friday 3 April AD33 (the 14th day of Nisan according to the Jewish calendar). The Ussher dating became widely used for some 300 years.

Archbishop Ussher

The amount of differences of the date assigned for Creation was calculated by Thomas Tegg (1776–1845) at 140 variations. Ussher, John Blair (d.1782) and Nicolas Dufresnoy (1674–1755) agreed on 4004BC; the Roman historian Josephus calculated it at 4658; the Samaritan Pentateuch 4700; the Talmud 5344; the Irish clergyman William Hales (1747–1831) 5411; and the Catholic Church has variously asserted 4000 and 4004.

The pair of dates that fit all the known facts for Christ's death are AD30 and 33; it took place at Passover on a Friday (the Gospels show that the next day was a Saturday, the Jewish Sabbath). This would mean Christ's death fell on the 14th or 15th of the Jewish month Nisan. (In the *Book of Exodus* God commanded the lamb to be slain on the 14th of Nisan, but the Jews in Jerusalem reckoned their days from sundown to sundown, leading to some disagreement as to when the 14th ended and the 15th began.)

The AD30 system co-existed with Ussher's and fixed the Crucifixion at 7 April AD30 (the 15th day of Nisan was also a Friday), and this date has now become the preferred estimate of modern scholars.

Chronological Atlas of the Bible has adopted this timeline.

In any such system of interpretation, inconsistencies occur, but it is indeed remarkable that in the two recognised accounts these vary in less than a span of 5 years – whether Creation or Crucifixion.

Published by
Third Millennium Press Ltd
Copyright © 2016 Third Millennium Press Ltd.,
Chippenham, England

Illustrations by permission of the Chamberlain Archive. Inquiries to reproduce illustrated material should be addressed to Third Millennium Press Ltd., Lowden Manor Cottage, Lowden Hill, Chippenham, Wiltshire, SN15 2BX, UK

ISBN: 978-1-86118-979-0

Designed by David Gibbons.
Printed in China.

CONTENTS

I The Old Testament: From the Deluge to Joseph

Noah's altar
Page 6 §1

The ark comes to rest on Mount Ararat. Page 6 §1

Abraham expels Hagar and Ishmael. Page 8 §7

Abraham prepares to sacrifice Isaac. Page 8 §9

Jacob cheats his brother Esau o[f] his inheritance. Page 10 §1

Joseph's sold to Ishmaelite slavers. Page 10 §17

Joseph interprets Pharaoh's dream. Page 14 §A

Joseph saves Egypt from famine. Page 14 §B

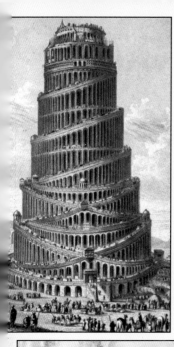

The Tower of Babel. Page 6 §2

Abram journeys from Ur. Page 6 §3

Abram and Lot. Page 8 §4

Joseph's coat of many colours. Page 10 §17

Jacob's dream of a ladder to Heaven. Page 10 §5

Jacob reunited with Joseph. Page 14 §C

Jacob's body taken to Hebron. Page 14 §C

1

NOAH AND THE DELUGE
Babel and Dispersion – Abraham and Lot
2347–1920BC

Genesis 6–13

1. MT. ARARAT. The history and geography of the Bible begin with the Deluge. Noah is 600 years old at this time and the date is B. C. 2347 The ark in which Noah and his family resided for a year and ten days landed on Ararat, a mountain 16.920 feet high. Soon after Noah had disembarked he built an altar and made a sacrifice to the Lord, which is the second altar mentioned in the Bible and the Lord promised by the rainbow that the earth should not be so destroyed again. Gen. 6-9.

2—BABEL. After the flood the race gradually pushed southward and one hundred years later the centre of population was Shinar and we find the people engaged in the building of a great city and tower which they called Babel. Shinar is some 500 miles from Mt. Ararat. Gen. 11.

THE DISPERSION. Apparently they had left God out of their calculations in building the city and tower and an end was put to the project by a confusion of their language and "The Lord scattered them abroad upon the face of all the earth." Ham migrated to what is now Palestine and Egypt. Jephtha moved north-west into what we now know as Asia Minor and finally into Europe while Shem remained in the region about the Tigris and Euphrates.

3—UR OF CHALDEA. Terah, a descendent of Shem is found, 247 years later, at U r o f Chaldea a n d Abram, his son is born there in 2001 B.C. (According to Ussher's system of dates Noah is still living.) Abram has two brothers, Haran and Nahor. Haron died in Chaldea leaving a son, Lot. Abram marries Sarai his half-sister and they adopt Lot. Gen. 11.

4—HARAN. About 1929 B. C. Terah moved up the Euphrates valley some 700 miles to a district called Haran and died there three years later at the age of 205.

5—SHECHEM. Abram now 75 years old took his share of the flocks and immediately started for an unknown country accompanied by Lot, and Nahor remained at Haran. He soon found himself at a place called Sichem (Shechem) 400 miles south-west of Haran. Here he built an altar which was his first the first built in the Holy Land and the third mentioned in the Bible. Gen. 12. (1926 B.C.)

6—BETHEL. Six years later we see Abram in Bethel about 20 miles south of Shechem where he built another altar, but a severe drought is in the land, his faith wavered and in his fear he took all his possessions and moved southward.

7—EGYPT. They finally found themselves in Egypt 300 miles south of Bethel where they received a hearty welcome until Abram, still under the spell of fear denied his wife to the king who was at the verge of taking her to be his wife, and the patriarch was expelled from the country. Pharaoh however was lenient with him, for although Abram was very rich the king did not confiscate his property and he returned to Bethel in Canaan and resumed his sacrifices on the altar he had left. Gen. 12-13 (1919).

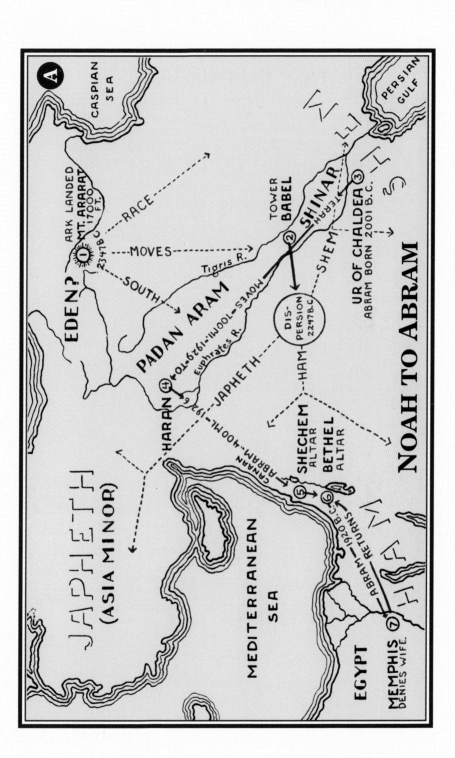

NOAH TO ABRAM

7

2

ABRAHAM AND ISAAC
The Great Promise
Beginning of Nations
1919–1846BC

Genesis 13–25

1—BETHEL. A quarrel between the herdsmen of Abram and Lot resulted in a separation of the two kinsmen and the latter moved over into the fertile valley of the Jordan near Sodom, about ten miles from Bethel.

2—HEBRON. Abram moves due south to Hebron (Mamre), a distance of 35 miles. Gen. 13.

2A—About five years later Lot is in Sodom and is captured by Chedorlaomer, an invading king and carried far into the north. Gen. 14.

3—DAN. Upon hearing of Lot's misfortune Abram summoned his servants and neighbours and started in pursuit, overtaking the marauders at Dan, 150 miles north.

4—HOBAH. The enemy was pursued with great loss to Hobah, 25 miles east and the king was slain, the property and Lot were recovered and they returned homeward.

5—KINGS DALE (JERUSALEM). Here Abram met the mysterious character, Melchizedek, king and priest of Salem and presented him with one tenth of the spoils which is the first mention of tithes in the Bible. Then Abram and Lot returned to their respective homes, Hebron and Sodom. Gen. 14.

6—HEBRON. Abram returned to Hebron from this expedition in 1918 B.C. and remained there for nearly 20 years. In the meantime God gave him the first great promise (1912) Ishmael was born, (1910) and in 1902 Isaac was promised and his name was changed from Abram to Abraham. Gen. 16.

2B—ZOAR. At this time Sodom was destroyed and only Lot and his two

daughters were saved. They found refuge at Zoar and his two sons Moab and Ammon were born. Gen. 19.

7—GERAR. Abraham moves to Gerar about 20 miles west. He is now 100 years old. (1901). Isaac is born and he again denies his wife, this time to king Abimelech. When Isaac was weaned Abraham expelled Hagar and Ishmael from his home and they went into the desert far to the south where they almost famished. Gen. 21 (see black line)

8—BEERSHEBA. The breach between Abraham and Abimelech widened and Abraham finally moved some 25 miles east where he dug a well and the two swore by it not to molest each other. They therefore called the place Beersheba, which means "well of the oath". Gen. 21. (1891 B.C.)

9—MORIAH. Abraham remained in Beersheba until Isaac was 25 (1874) when he was tempted to make a burnt offering of his son in the Land of Moriah (later the site of Solomon's temple) but he was interrupted by an angel and did not make the sacrifice. He returned to Beersheba where he remained many years. Gen. 22, 23.

10—HEBRON. Then Abraham moved to Hebron again and Sarah died there (1860) and was buried in the Cave Machpelah. Isaac, now 40, married Rebecca a grand-daughter of Nahor of Haran (see black line 11). After this Abraham married Keturah who bore him six children. Midian was the outstanding one who migrated to Arabia (black line 12). Abraham died in Hebron at the age of 175 and was buried in the Cave Machpelah by the side of Sarah. Gen. 24, 25. 1825 B.C.

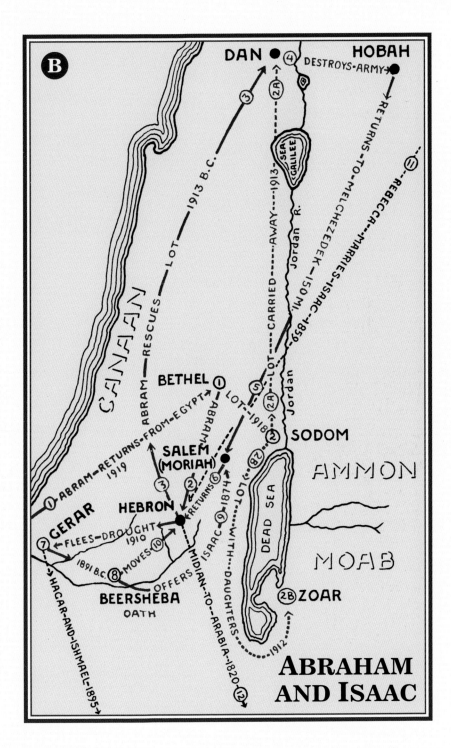

B

DAN HOBAH
DESTROYS ARMY

LOT 1913 B.C.
ABRAM RESCUES

SEA GALILEE

CARRIED AWAY 1913

Jordan R. 150 MI.

RETURNS TO MELCHEZEDEK

REBECCA MARRIES ISAAC 1859

CANAAN

ABRAM RETURNS FROM EGYPT 1919

BETHEL

SALEM (MORIAH)

Jordan

LOT 1918

SODOM

GERAR

HEBRON

RETURNS 1917

AMMON

DEAD SEA

FLEES DROUGHT 1910

MOVES

1891 B.C.

OFFERS ISAAC

MIDIAN TO ARABIA 1820

MOAB

BEERSHEBA OATH

LOT WITH DAUGHTERS

ZOAR

1912

HAGAR AND ISHMAEL 1895

ABRAHAM AND ISAAC

9

3 ISAAC – JACOB – JOSEPH
Renewal of Promise – The New Man
1846–1729BC

Genesis 25–37

1—LAHAROI. Isaac now lives in Laharoi and Ishmael in the great wilderness of Paran fifty miles south of him but they meet together in Hebron to bury Abraham, their father, and then return to their respective homes. Isaac's twins. Esau and Jacob, are born at Laharoi (1844) and Jacob barters Esau's birthright fifteen years later. Gen. 25.

2—GERAR. Isaac now moves to Gerar where he denies his wife as his father had done and he is evicted from Abimelech's city and dwells by the river fifteen miles east (3) and from thence he moves to Beersheba (4) where God renews with him the promise he had made to Abraham. Gen. 26.

5—HEBRON. Later we find Isaac in Hebron again; he is old and blind and is deceived into letting Jacob rob Esau of his blessing. Because of the cunning of his mother and the fear of Esau, Jacob flees to Bethel (6) in 1804 B.C. and simultaneously Esau goes to Edom (7). Bethel is 35 miles north of Hebron and here Jacob tarries for some time. Here the ladder was let down from heaven in a dream and he called the place the "House of God." (Bethel) Gen. 27.

8—HARAN. From Bethel Jacob pushed on toward Padan-Aram (Haran). He married the daughters (Rachel and Leah) of Laban and there were born to him 11 boys and one daughter during the twenty years he remained there. Jacob slipped away by night and had been gone several days before his absence was discovered. Gen. 28-31.

9—MAHANEUM. Laban overtook him at Mahaneum in Gilead. He was seeking his lost idols which he believed Jacob had taken, but which he failed to find among his baggage. They separated good friends and Laban re-

turned to Haran and we never hear of him any more. Jacob sent presents from here to Esau in Edom for he feared him, but Esau had already started to meet him. Gen. 31 (1740 B.C.)

10—PENUEL. On the banks of Jabbok (Penuel) Jacob prays all night, receives the blessing. his name is changed to ISRAEL (Prevails with God) and next morning meets Esau (11) only to find that he has been his friend all the time. Gen. 32, 33.

12—SUCCOTH. Jacob next moves to Succoth where he remains for a time and does some building. Gen. 33.

13—SHECHEM. Jacob buys land and digs a well at Shechem. he finds Rachel with the idols which he buries, and following a battle between his sons and the natives he moves southward to Bethel (14). Deborah, Rachels nurse, and one of his wives dies here.

15—EPHRATH. (Bethlehem). When he arrived at Ephrath Benjamin was born and Rachel died and Jacob buried her by the road-side. Gen. 35.

16—HEBRON. Hebron, his old home is only 15 miles south and when he arrived he found his father still living. Isaac lived to the age of 180 (1724) and Esau and Jacob buried him in the cave Machpelah by the side of his father, Abraham. Gen. 36.

17—DOTHAN. Joseph was his father's preference and the other brothers hated him. Jacob sent the boy to Shechem on an errand to his sons, but not finding them there he finally located them at Dothan. The jealous brothers sold him to a band of Ishmaelitish traders who carried him into Egypt (18) where he was sold into slavery. Gen. 37. (1729 B.C.)

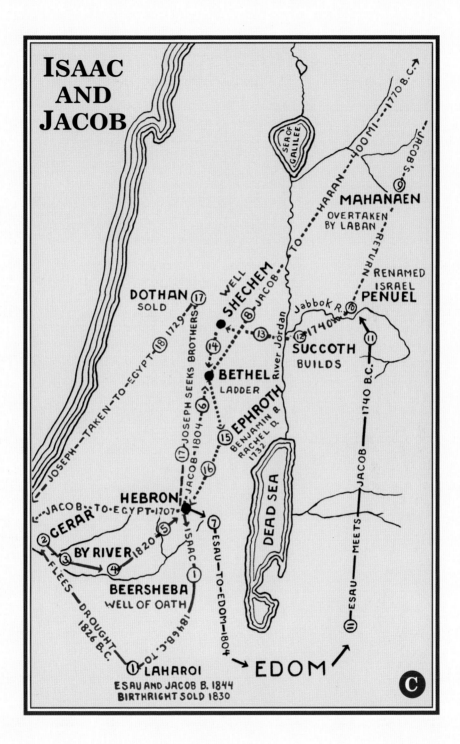

ISAAC AND JACOB

DOTHAN SOLD

SEA OF GALILEE

MAHANAEN OVERTAKEN BY LABAN

JACOB'S — 1770 B.C.

400 MI — TO HARAN

RETURN — RENAMED ISRAEL PENUEL

WELL SHECHEM

⑨

JACOB

⑧ JACOB

Jabbok R.

⑬

⑫ 1740 B.C.

⑩

⑪ 1740 B.C.

SUCCOTH BUILDS

⑰

JOSEPH — TAKEN — TO — EGYPT — 1729

⑱ 1729

⑭

JOSEPH SEEKS BROTHERS

JACOB — 1804

⑰

⑬

BETHEL LADDER

⑥

EPHROTH BENJAMIN B. RACHEL D. 1732

⑮

⑯

River Jordan

DEAD SEA

HEBRON

JACOB — TO — EGYPT — 1707

GERAR

②

③

BY RIVER 1820

⑤

④

ISAAC

⑦

ESAU — TO — EDOM — 1804

FLEES

ESAU — MEETS — JACOB

⑪

BEERSHEBA WELL OF OATH

①

DROUGHT 1826 B.C. TO

① LAHAROI

ESAU AND JACOB B. 1844 BIRTHRIGHT SOLD 1830

EDOM

ⓒ

11

II The Old Testament: The Exodus and the Promised Land

Moses found among the bulrushes. Page 14 §1

The burning bush. Page 14 §1

The plague of flies. Page 14 §2

Gathering manna. Page 14 §7

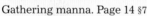

The golden calf. Page 14 §9

Moses conjures water from the rocks. Page 14 §8

Crossing the Jordan. Page 16 §5

Judge Deborah. Page 18 §6

Samson slays the lion. Page 20 §19

Painting the lintel
at Passover. Page 14 §2

Death of the first-born. Page 14 §2

The Egyptian army destroyed
by the waters. Page 14 §4

Moses smashes the tablets of
the Ten Commandments.
Page 14 §9

The brazen serpent.
Page 16 §17

The Return of the spies.
Page 16 §4

Gideon's night attack.
Page 20 §12

Samson pulls down
the Philistine pillars.
Page 20 §23

Ruth and Naomi. Page 20 §24

4 MOSES
1727–1452BC
Genesis 40 – Numbers 21

A—EGYPT. Joseph arrived in Egypt probably Memphis) about 1729 B.C. and was sold to Potiphar but within eleven years, he was falsely accused by the officer's wife and cast into prison. He had been incarcerated about three years when he interpreted the king's dream to be a prediction of a great drought which would begin seven years hence. Joseph was then given his liberty and elevated to high office and through his efforts the whole country was saved as well as his father's family in Canaan. (Gen. 40-41).

B—ON. Pharaoh arranged the wedding of Joseph and Asenath, daughter of the priest of On and their two sons were Ephraim and Manasseh. The famine came as Joseph had predicted and "was severe in all the land" but they had plenty and to spare. (Gen. 41).

C—HEBRON. Jacob still resides in Hebron and the drought reached him also; he sent his sons to Egypt for food and as a result he was finally taken there himself and found his son whom he had supposed dead, to be alive and holding a position second only to the king himself. (Gen. 41-46) (1707 B.C.). Pharaoh turned over the land of Goshen to Jacob's family. After living there for eighteen years Jacob died and was taken under military escort (D) to Hebron for burial. (Gen. 47-50) (1689). Joseph continued his good work for fifty-four years after his father's death and at the age of one hundred and ten, died. (1635). He requested a burial at Shechem which was carried out nearly three hundred years later.

1—MEMPHIS. About one hundred years after Joseph's death, Moses was born near Memphis and his life was saved by Pharaoh's daughter. His fist act at the age of forty was to sympathize with his people and as a result of slaying an Egyptian taskmaster for his cruelty to a kinsman, he was compelled to flee the country. (Ex. 1-2). (1531 B.C.). Moses fled to Midian, South of Mt. Sinai, and engaged as a shepherd with Jethro, a priest and distant relative, and afterward he married the priest's daughter, Zipporah. Their sons were Gershom and Eliezer. While attending the flocks near Mt. Horeb (Sinai) "I

AM THAT I AM", GOD. directed him to return to Egypt and deliver Israel. (Ex. 2-3) (1492).

2—RAMSES. In response to his command, Moses returned to Egypt and after an encounter with Pharaoh which must have lasted for several weeks, and resulting in ten terrible plagues, the yoke of bondage was thrown off and six-hundred and sixty thousand men started for Canaan during the night of the Passover and the death of the first born of Egypt.

3—SUCCOTH. Their first stop was Succoth where the pillar of cloud by day and light by night, appeared to them and continued to lead them for forty years. (Ex. 13).

4—BAAL-ZEPHON. They approached the sea about forty miles south, opposite Baal-Zephon and there Pharaoh's army overtook them. Here the sea opened and Israel crossed dry-shod but when the Egyptians pursued them into the sea, they were swallowed up by the inrushing waters. When they were safe on the other side Miriam composed a song and sang it and all Israel joined with her (Ex. 13-15).

5—MARAH. They started south along the shore of the Red Sea and first stopped at Marah (Bitter Water) and Moses sweetened the water by a miracle. (Ex. 15).

6—ELIM. The next stop was Elim where there was plenty of water and seventy palm trees, ten miles south of Marah.

7—WILDERNESS OF SIN. A few miles south of Elim they enter the Wildness of Sin. Here they are given manna for food which never ceased during the sojourn, and quail for this particular time. (Num. 16). They have been free just six weeks.

8—REPHIDIM. At Rephidim Moses brought water from the rock. They were attacked by Amalek who was defeated and Jethro, accompanied by Moses' wife and two sons, came to meet them here. (Num. 17-18).

9—SINAI. Israel arrives at the foot of Mt. Sinai, two hundred miles from Goshen after three months of hazardous travel. Moses goes up into the mountain where he obtains the law on tables of stone. During his absence, Aaron casts a gold calf and Moses breaks the tablets when he discovers

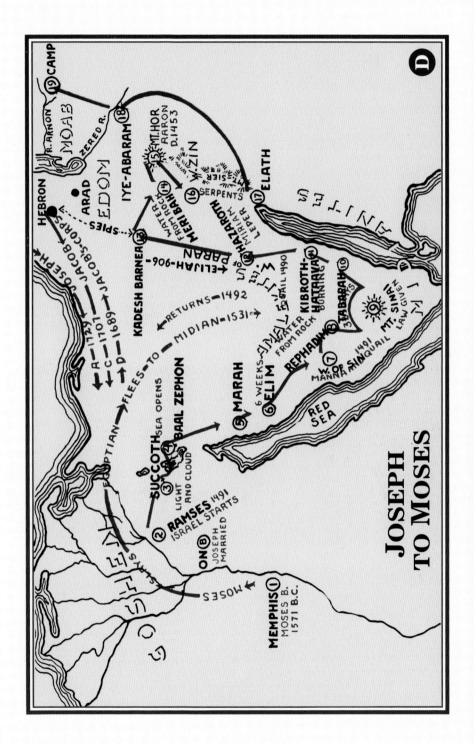

JOSEPH TO MOSES

15

Israel's idolatry. He then returns and after another forty days he comes down with other tablets, and explicit directions for the construction of the tabernacle, the Ark of the Covenant and a general code of civil and religious laws. (Num. 18-34).

10—TABERAH. The pillar of cloud and light is still present. They have been camped at Sinai three-hundred twenty-five days. The cloud rises and directs them first to Taberah in the Wilderness of Paran where many complain and are consumed by fire. Taberah means "Burning". (Num. 9-10).

11—KIBROTH-HATTAAVA. Here the people murmured about their food, and quail were sent and they ate of them until thousands of people died of gluttony. It has been just a year since the quail came over the first time. Kibroth-Hattaava means "Graves of Lust." (Num. 11).

12—HAZEROTH. Miriam and Aaron conspire against Moses and Miriam contracts leprosy but·she is healed by Moses. From here they make a long march to Kadesh-Barnea. (Num. 12).

13—KADESH-BARNEA. From Kadesh-Barnea. Israel wandered about various parts for thirty-eight years.

Spies were sent into Canaan and proceeded as far as Hebron, (Valley of Eshicol. Korah instituted a rebellion, Aaron's rod budded and Miriam died. (Num. 12-19).

14—WILDERNESS OF ZIN. Moses again brings water from the rock in the Wilderness of Zin, and the place is called Meribah. Both Moses and Aaron are deprived of entering the Promised Land because of their attitude upon this occasion. Aaron dies immediately and is buried in Mt. Hor (15) and Eleazar, his son, inherits his office. (Num. 20). The king of Arad now comes down and attacks Israel but is repulsed. (Num. 21).

17—ELATH. Because Edom refuses to let Israel pass through their territory, they turn south and encompass the land of Edom via. Elath. During this journey they are bitten by serpents and Moses heals them by raising the serpent of brass. (16) Num. 21).

19—RIVER ARNON. From Elath they turn north around Mt. Sier and only halt at Oboth, Ije-abarim (18) and the Zered. Then they obtain permission to pass through Moab and camp on the river Arnon. (Num. 21). (1452 B. C.).

5 JOSHUA AND THE CONQUEST OF CANAAN 1451–1427BC

Book of Joshua

1—JAHAZ. Before Moses moved north from the Arnon, he sent messengers to Sihon, king of the Amorites at Heshbon (2) to ask permission to pass through his domains to the Jordan. The king not only refused his request but he met Israel at Jahaz with armed forces but they were annihilated and Sihon himself was killed with them. And they camped near the Jordan (3) (Num. 21).

4—EDREI. The northern Amorites were under the giant king, Og. Moses marched against him at Edrei and there was another total defeat of the enemy which gave to Israel the entire country east of the Jordan. (Num. 21).

3—JORDAN. They then returned to their camp at the Fords of Jordan where Moses read all the law to them, delivered his farewell address and turned his commission over to Joshua. (Num. 21).

A. During this time the march

against Midian resulting from Baalam's evil intention to curse Israel by some kind of charm. took a portion of the army to Moab where the Midianites were annihilated and Baalam also lost his life with them. (Num. 22-25).

—MT NEBO. Moses then retired to Mt. Nebo where he died and was buried by the hand of the Lord, and no one has ever seen his grave. (Deut. 34:5-7. B. C. 1451). Immediately Joshua sent spies to Jericho, across the Jordan ten miles west, who brought back encouraging reports. (Joshua 2).

5—GILGAL. Then Joshua decided to cross the river into Canaan; here the waters of the Jordan parted and Israel crossed on dry land. Joshua at once built an altar, constructing it from twelve stones which had been gathered from the bed of the Jordan when they crossed it. Then he circumcised every male, held a passover

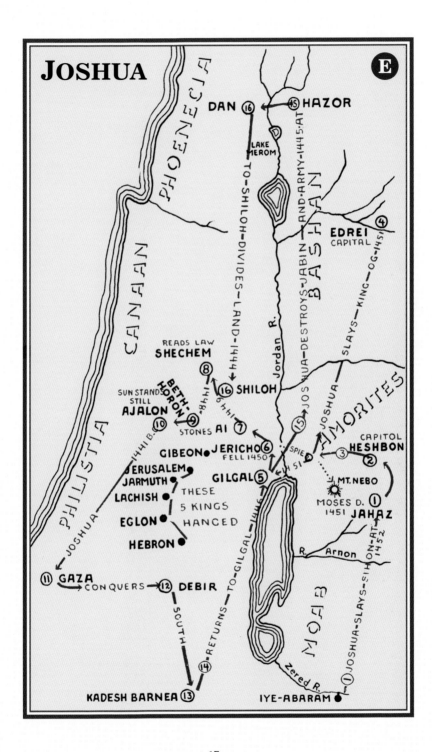

JOSHUA

E

PHOENECIA

DAN 16   15 HAZOR

LAKE MEROM

CANAAN

TO—SHILOH—DIVIDES—LAND—1444

Jordan R.

JOSHUA—DESTROYS—JABIN AND ARMY—1445 AT

BASHAN

EDREI CAPITAL 4

SLAYS—KING—OG—1451

AMORITES

READS LAW
SHECHEM

8

SHILOH 16

BETH-HORON

SUN STANDS STILL
AJALON

10

STONES

AI 7

9

JOSHUA

GIBEON   JERICHO 6

SPIE

CAPITOL
HESHBON

3   2

JERUSALEM
JARMUTH

GILGAL 5

MT. NEBO

FELL 1450

15

PHILISTIA

LACHISH

THESE

MOSES D.
1451

1

5 KINGS

EGLON

HANGED

JAHAZ

HEBRON

R. Arnon

11 GAZA

MOAB

CONQUERS 12 DEBIR

JOSHUA—SLAYS—SIHON—AT—1452

SOUTH

RETURNS—TO—GILGAL

14

KADESH BARNEA 13

IYE-ABARAM

Zered R.

1 JOSHUA—SLAYS—

feast and the manna they had fed upon for forty years ceased to fall. (Joshua 4-5).

6—JERICHO. Joshua's first move was to attack Jericho, under the direction of an angel. All the inhabitants (except Rahab) were put to the sword, the walls fell and not a house was left standing in the entire city. (Joshua 6).

7—AI. Two attempts were made before Ai was taken. The first failed on account of Achan who stole the golden wedge from the plunder of Jericho. (Joshua 8).

8—SHECHEM. After the capitulation of Ai, Joshua led the army to Shechem, erected an altar and read the cursings and blessings of the Law and the people responded with a hearty 'Amen'. (Joshua 8).

—GIBEON. The Gibeonites fearing Israel after they had seen these marvelous victories, came to Joshua with a proposition of peace and the great leader covenanted with them before he had discovered that they were deceiving him. (Joshua 9).

—JERUSALEM, HEBRON, JARMUTH, LACHISH, EGLON. The allied kings of these five cities hearing of the Gibeon league came against them, led by Adoni-Bezek, king of Jerusalem. But Joshua came from Gilgal to their rescue in spite of the fact that they had deceived him, and the armies of these kings were put to flight. (Joshua 9).

9—BETH-HORAN. The five kings were repulsed to Beth-Horan where thousands of their ranks were destroyed by a rain of stones. (Joshua 10).

10—VALLEY OF AJALON. The remnant of their army was pressed westward to Ajalon where Joshua commanded the sun to stay his course until he had finished with the enemy and the allies were completely destroyed. The five kings were hanged and their five cities fell to Israel. (Joshua 10).

11—GAZA. Joshua now proceeded against Gaza, then to Debir (12) and Kadesh-Barnea (13) and at the conclusion of this campaign he returned to Gilgal. (line 14).

15—LAKE MEROM. Jabin, king of Hazor. in the north. now advanced against Joshua and they met at Lake Merom. Jabin's army was beaten back to Hazor. The king was put to death and the city and chariots burned. (Joshua 10).

16—SHILOH. Thus Joshua had mastered the whole land of Canaan, having destroyed thirty-one kings during the seven year's campaign, he came to Shiloh where the land was divided among the tribes, 1444 B.C. as shown on the next map.

6 DEBORAH – GIDEON – SAMSON
1427–1142BC
Book of Judges

1—BEZEK. Israel had no king, but judges were raised up at various times to direct the people and put down local disturbances and the book of Judges relates some of the incidents. The first was at Bezek which was taken by Judah. The king of Jerusalem, Adoni-Bezek, happened to be there at this time and was also captured. Judges 1.

2—DEBIR. Othneil took Debir and various other cities fell to Judah, as reported in Judges 1 to 3. Othneil also checked the mesopotamian advance and became the first judge of Israel. Judges 3.

3—GILGAL. Eglon, king of Moab, who attempted to intrude himself upon Israel, was murdered at Gilgal where he maintained a temporary residence for the purpose of collecting a tribute he assessed upon them without any apparent reason. Judges 3.

6—HAZOR. At this time there is a well organized attempt at Hazor to occupy the country about Mt. Carmel. Sisera was sent there to protect their interests and Deborah, who was a judge at Mt. Ephraim, (4) summoned Barak of Kadesh (5) to meet her at Mt. Tabor (7) with ten thousand men and they advanced against Sisera and destroyed his entire army in the Valley of the Kishon (8). Judges 4.

9—Megiddo. Sisera fled for his life to Megiddo but he was slain there by a Kenite woman, Jael, and the revolt was put down. Judges 4.

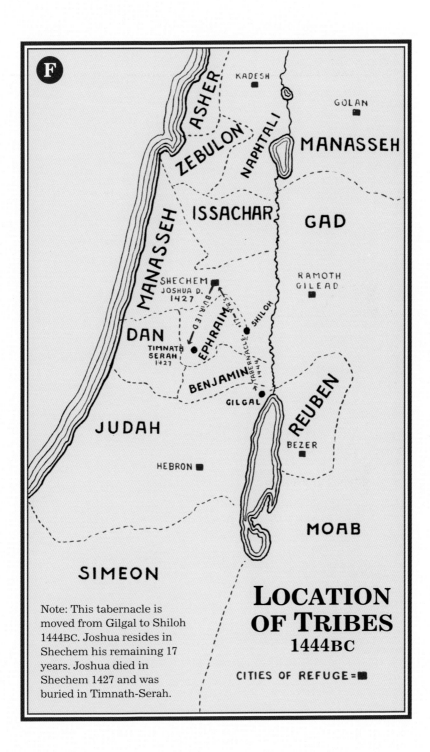

F

KADESH

GOLAN

ASHER

ZEBULON

NAPHTALI

MANASSEH

ISSACHAR

GAD

MANASSEH

SHECHEM
JOSHUA D.
1427

BURIED

RAMOTH
GILEAD

DAN

EPHRAIM

SHILOH

TIMNATH
SERAH
1427

TABERNACLE 1444

BENJAMIN

REUBEN

GILGAL

JUDAH

BEZER

HEBRON

MOAB

SIMEON

LOCATION OF TRIBES
1444BC

CITIES OF REFUGE = ■

Note: This tabernacle is moved from Gilgal to Shiloh 1444BC. Joshua resides in Shechem his remaining 17 years. Joshua died in Shechem 1427 and was buried in Timnath-Serah.

19

12—MIDIAN. Marauders from Midian and Amalek had been robbing Israel of her crops in the territory of Mt. Gilboa. Gideon was called from Oph-rah (10) and with his famous "torch and pitcher brigade" literally fright-ened thousands of them to death near the foot of Gilboa and drove the dis-organized army across the Jordan: first to Succoth (13), then to Penuel (14) and finally to Karkor (15). One hundred and twenty thousand were slain and their kings Zebah and Zal-munna were beheaded. Judges 7 (B.C. 1249).

16—TIRZAH. Abimelech, son of Gid-eon, now takes advantage of his fath-er's popularity and makes himself king in Shechem, but in his attempt to subdue Tirzah, a woman dropped a mill-stone on his head and rather than die at the hand of a woman, he ord-ered his armour bearer to stab him to death. Judges 9.

17—TOB. Then marauders began pil-laging the granaries east of the Jor-dan and Jephtha was called upon to clear the country of them as Gideon had done on the west. He drove the Ammonites into the desert, but be-cause of a rash vow he had made, he felt called upon to make a burnt offer-ing of his daughter. Jephtha judged Israel six years. Judges 11 (1207 B.C.).

18—ZORAH. We next come to the ex-ploits of the eccentric Samson who was born at Zorah, 1250 B.C. Judges 13.

19—TIMNATH. He married a Philis-tine woman (Deliliah) at Timnath. He was a very strong man and once while on his way to Timnath he encountered a lion and slew it by the sheer force of his hands. Later he passed the lion's carcass and bees had hived in it and he ate of the honey.

20—ASKELON. At his wedding, Sam-son made a riddle of the incidents. Through the unfaithfulness of his wife, who gave the answer out to thirty Philistines who heard the riddle, it cost him the bet he had made which was a suit of clothes for each one, and Samson went to Askelon and slew thirty Philistines, took their clothes and paid the wager.

PLAIN OF SHARON. In the mean-time Samson's wife was given to an-other man and in retaliation he fired the Philistines' crops on the Plain of Sharon by the use of foxes and red-hot firebrands. Judges 15.

21—ETAM—After this incident he hid himself at Etam, but was captured and tied with ropes which he broke like "ropes of ashes".

22—LEHI. He then fled to Lehi. He picked up the jawbone of the skeleton of an ass and slew a thousand of the Philistines and escaped.

23—GAZA. Then he went into Gaza, the capitol, and when they attempted to shut him in the city he lifted the gate from the wall of the city and carried it over near Hebron. (24) twenty-five or thirty miles east. His last act was to pull the great temple of Gaza down upon himself and thous-ands of merrymakers and they were all killed and Samson was carried back to Zorah for burial by his brothers and father. Judges 16.

24—DAN. The 18th chapter tells of the 600 who went to Laish (Dan) in the extreme north and established a new religious cult.

25—GIBEAH. Judges 19-21 tells a gruesome story of a Bethlehem woman killed by the Benjamites at Gibeah, their slaughter for the crime and the capture of the girls at Shiloh.

24—MOAB. Then comes the story of Ruth who was born in Moab, was brought to Bethlehem by Naomi, mar-ried Boaz and became the great grandmother of David and of course the great ancestress of Jesus. Ruth 1-4 (1312 B.C.).

26—RAMAH. Samuel was born about 1160 B.C. and was dedicated to the Lord at Shiloh (27) when he was weaned. He was under the tutorage of Eli, the devout priest, for nearly twenty years. Eli fell dead when he learned that his two sons had lost their lives in battle and the ark had been captured by the Philistines (1142 B.C.) 1 Sam. 1-4.

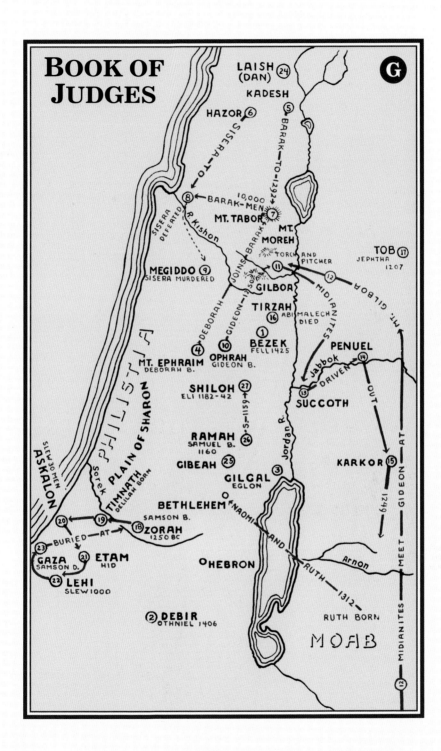

BOOK OF JUDGES

LAISH (DAN) 24
KADESH
HAZOR 6
BARAK-TO 1292 5
SISERA-TO
SISERA DEFEATED
R. Kishon
8 BARAK-MEN 10,000
MT. TABOR 7
MT. MOREH
TORCH AND PITCHER
TOB 17 JEPHTHA 1207
11
12
MT. GILBOA
MEGIDDO 9 SISERA MURDERED
GILBOA
JOINS BARAK
DEBORAH
GIDEON
TIRZAH 16 ABIMALECH DIED
MIDIANITES
1 BEZEK FELL 1425
4
10 OPHRAH GIDEON B.
PENUEL
MT. EPHRAIM DEBORAH B.
Jabbok
DRIVEN
14
SHILOH 27 ELI 1182-42
13 SUCCOTH
OUT
S-1159
RAMAH SAMUEL B. 1160
26
Jordan R.
KARKOR 15
GIBEAH
29
1249
GILGAL 3 EGLON
MEET GIDEON AT
PLAIN OF SHARON
Sorek
TIMNATH DELILAH BORN
BETHLEHEM
NAOMI AND
20 19 18 ZORAH 1250 BC
SAMSON B.
BURIED AT
Arnon
23 21 ETAM HID
GAZA SAMSON D.
HEBRON
RUTH 1312
22 LEHI SLEW 1000
PHILISTIA
ASKALON SLEW 30 MEN
2 DEBIR OTHNIEL 1406
RUTH BORN
MOAB
MIDIANITES
12

III The Old Testament: The Kingdoms and Captivities of Israel

David and Goliath. Page 24 §16

David cuts the hem of Saul's garment. Page 24 §23

Saul visits the Witch of Endor. Page 26 §27

Rehoboam divides the Kingdom. Page 28 §1

Elijah saves the Widow's son. Page 28 §13

Elijah defeats the prophets of Baal. Page 28 §14

Josiah discovers the lost book of the Law. Page 32 §15

Esther and King Xerxes. Page 32

David becomes the King of Israel. Page 26 §1

The Ark of the Covenant brought to Jerusalem by King David. Page 26 §8

Absalom usurps the throne. Page 26 §10

The death of Jezebel. Page 28 §18

Elijah taken up to Heaven. Page 30 §21

Elisha and the Shunammite. Page 30 §24

Nehemiah rebuilds the walls of Jerusalem. Page 32

Daniel and Nebuchadnezzar. Page 32

7 SAUL AND DAVID
The Rise of the Kingdom – Samuel the Prophet
1442–1056BC

I Samuel 1–31

1—SHILOH. The ark of the covenant which was taken from Shiloh and is now in Philistine territory was first brought to Ashdod (2) then to Gath (3) Ekron (4) and Bethshemesh (5) and its presence brought destruction and death in each place. The Philistines were glad to release it and it was taken to Kirjath-Jearim (6) where it remained until David took Jerusalem. 1 Sam. 5-7.

7—RAMAH. Samuel now lives at Ramah. A young Benjamite named Saul happened through Ramah on an errand for his father and Samuel suddenly anointed him King of Israel. 1 Sam. 9-10.

8—MIZPAH. Samuel immediately summoned Israel to Mizpah and they all confirmed his choice. 1 Sam. 10 (B.C. 1095).

9—JABESH-GILEAD. Saul's first act was to clear the east Jordan tribes of the Ammonites and when he did this they also accepted him in a great demonstration at Gilgal (10) 1 Sam. 10-11.

11—GEBA. After the siege of Geba, the Philistines were reinforced at Michmash (12) and they so frightened Israel that the army deserted Jonathan, son of Saul their leader. Samuel was to have met Saul at Gilgal to offer sacrifices but because of his belated arrival Saul Officiated at the altar himself and Samuel denounced him and predicted that his rule would soon come to an end. 1 Sam. 13.

13—AMALEKITES. Saul is now directed to slay all the Amalekites in South Palestine,—every man, woman and child. He did so, except that he brought Agag, the King to Gilgale, alive. This so incensed Samuel that he denounced Saul again and "hewed Agag to pieces" with his own hand and Samuel never saw Saul again. 1 Sam. 15 (1079 B.C.).

14—BETHLEHEM. Samuel then went to Bethlehem and anointed David, a mere shepherd boy, to succeed Saul. David was a musician, and the King having been seized with fits of melancholy sent for him to come to Gibeah, the capital, (15) and play for him, but

Saul could not have been aware of Samuel's visit and mission for "he loved David and made him his armour bearer." 1 Sam. 16 (1065 B.C.).

16—ELAH. At this time Saul throws his whole military force with Judah against the Philistines in the Valley of Elah. and the lad, David, is sent on an errand by his father to the front which is only a few miles from Bethlehem. While he was there, though he was not a soldier, he slew the insultant Goliath, a giant from Gath (3) 1 Sam. 17 (1063 B.C.).

17—NOB. This incident "knit the soul of Jonathan to David" and they covenated everlasting friendship, but it infuriated Saul, his father, who had probably heard of David's anointing by this time and the King tried to destroy him. But Saul's daughter, Michal, whom David had married in the meantime assisted him in his escape and he fled to Nob, (17) the city of the priests nearby. 1 Sam. 21.

19—ADULLAM. From Nob David went to Gath, (3), former home of Goliath, but the King, Achish, evidently recognized him and the boy barely escaped with his life and hid himself in a cave at Adullam. 1 Sam. 21. Saul killed 80 priests at Nob for harbouring the fugative, David, and in the meantime David sent his own father to Moab (20) for safety. He then gathered a band of 600 men at Ziph (21) for protection. 1 Sam. 22.

22—MAON. Saul heard about this and led his army against David but the youth by this time had escaped to Maon and from there to Engedi. 1 Sam. 23.

23—ENGEDI. Saul kept trailing him and here at Engedi David slipped into Saul's tent and cut off a part of the King's garment while he slept but did not harm him. and Saul was so embarrassed that he returned home. In the meantime Samuel died and was buried in Mizpah. (8). 1 Sam. 24 (1060 B.C.).

24—CARMEL. David then came to Carmel and married Abigail, the widow of Nabal, for Saul had given Michal his first wife to Phalti of Laish,

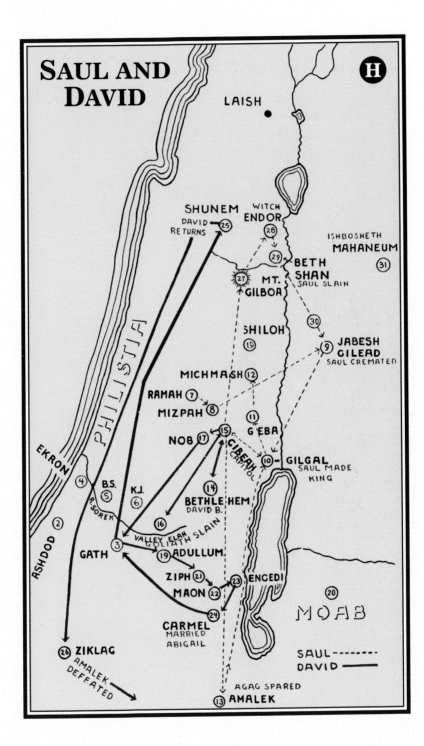

SAUL AND DAVID

LAISH

SHUNEM
DAVID
RETURNS
25

WITCH
ENDOR
28

MAHANEUM
ISHBOSHETH
31

29
BETH
SHAN
SAUL SLAIN

27
MT.
GILBOA

30

SHILOH
19

JABESH
GILEAD
SAUL CREMATED
9

MICHMASH 12

RAMAH 7
MIZPAH 8

11
GEBA

NOB 17
15
GIBEAH
CAPITOL
10
GILGAL
SAUL MADE
KING

PHILISTIA

EKRON

B.S.
5
R. SOREK
K.J.
6

14

BETHLEHEM
DAVID B.

4

ASHDOD

2

16

3
VALLEY ELAH
GOLIATH SLAIN

GATH
19 ADULLUM

ZIPH 21
MAON 22
23
ENGEDI

24

20

MOAB

CARMEL
MARRIED
ABIGAIL

26 ZIKLAG
AMALEK
DEFEATED

SAUL - - - - -
DAVID

AGAG SPARED
13 AMALEK

H

25

a city in the north. 1 Sam. 25 (1059 B.C.).

25—SHUMEN. David returned to King Achish of Gath (3) and he and his gang were accepted and added to the Philistine army and they all advanced to Shumen and waited for Saul's army to arrive for a fight to the finish. 1 Sam. 28.

26—ZIKLAG. But the Amalekites were again stirring up trouble in the south, so David was sent back to Ziklag by Achish where he annihilated them. 1 Sam. 30.

27—MT. GILBOA. In the meantime Saul arrived at Mt. Gilboa. He then visited the Witch of Endor (28) who predicted his death which occurred the next day at the Battle of Bethshan (29) where Saul and his sons, (except Ishbosheth, a cripple) were beheaded and their bodies hung on the walls of the city. 1 Sam. 31.

30—JABESH-GILEAD. The people over at Jabesh-Gilead whom Saul had favoured years before, cut his body down from the wall and cremated it in that city. 1 Sam. 31 (1056 B. C.).

31—MAHANEUM. Abner, Saul's commander-in-chief, took Ishbosheth to Mahaneum and attempted to rally the people to his support as King but the response was a very feeble one.

DAVID AND SOLOMON
The Kingdom Established
1056–975BC

I Samuel – Kings 10

1—ZIKLAG. David had returned to Ziklag when he heard of the death of Saul so he ignored Achish and brought the spoils of the Amalekites direct to Hebron (2) and distributed them among his own people who immediately crowned him king of Judah. 2 Sam. 1, 2. (1056 B.C.).

3—GIBEON. At this time Abner arranged a pretended peace conference with Joab, David's military leader, at Gibeon, but the trickster intended taking Joab's life, and did slay his brother and escaped. But later Joab stabbed him "under the fifth rib" at Hebron during a visit he was making with David. In the meantime Ishbosheth was beheaded and his murderers were hanged over the pool of Hebron by David. David is now proclaimed king of all Israel by all the tribes at the age of 30, after he had ruled Judah for 7½ years. 2 Sam. 3, 4. (1048 B.C.).

4—JERUSALEM. Immediately following this, Joab takes Jerusalem and David makes it his capitol. King Hiram of Tyre (16) helps him to rebuild and beautify the city and constructs a palace for him on Mt. Zion. 2 Sam. 5.

5—GATH. King Achish of Gath, stung by David's infiedlity came against Jerusalem at Rephaim (6) but was driven back with great loss to Gezer (7) on the plain of Sharon.

8—KIRJATH-JEARIM. David then moved the Ark of the Covenant from Kirjath-Jearim where it had been for 20 years, to Jerusalem and placed it in a new tabernacle he had set up on Ophal. 2 Sam. 6.

9—GESHER. About this time Absalom killed his brother Amnon who had abused a sister and through his death Absalom became heir to the throne which he coveted. He fled to his grandfather, king of Gesher, but after 3 years a reconciliation was effected by Joab and he returned to Jerusalem. In the meantime David had Uriah murdered and then married his widow, Bath-Sheba. 2 Sam. 7-15.

10—MAHANEUM. The pampered son (Absalom) moved to Hebron (2) and instituted a rebellion against his father and David fled to Mahaneum. He was pursued by Absalom who was slain by Joab and then David returned to Jerusalem. 2 Sam. 15-19. (1023 B.C.). A great celebration was given for him as he passed through Gilgal and the people reassured David of their allegiance to him.

11—BETHLEHEM. Again the people of Gath waged war against David but a decisive victory over them at Bethlehem drove them home and the trouble was forever ended. 2 Sam. 21.

David died in Jerusalem (1015 B.C.) at the age of 70, after a rule of 40 years and he was buried on Mt. Zion. (see map S.) His much enlarged kingdom extended from the Euphrates to the rivers of Egypt and from the Mediterranean to the gulf of Akabah. (For the scope of this territory see map K). He was succeeded by his son Solomon, the son of Bath-Sheba. 1 Kings 2.

Solomon came to the throne at a time of peace and aside from a few local disturbances there were no mili-

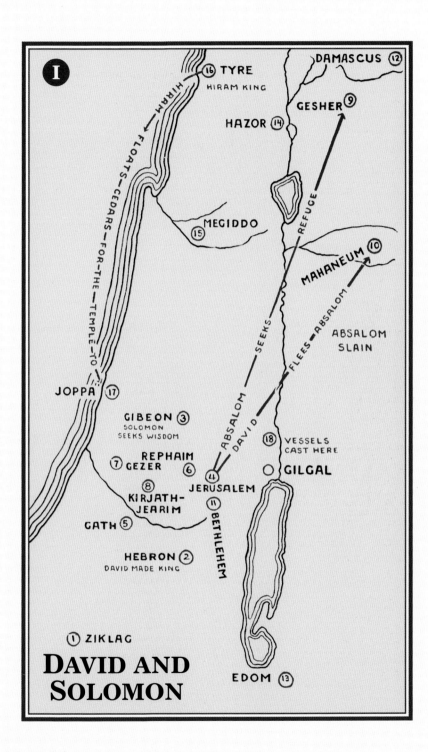

I

DAMASCUS (12)

(16) TYRE
HIRAM KING

GESHER (9)

HAZOR (14)

HIRAM

FLOATS—CEDARS—FOR—THE—TEMPLE—TO

MEGIDDO

(15)

REFUGE

MAHANEUM

(10)

ABSALOM
SLAIN

JOPPA (17)

GIBEON (3)
SOLOMON
SEEKS WISDOM

ABSALOM SEEKS

DAVID

FLEES—ABSALOM

(7) REPHAIM
GEZER (6)

(18) VESSELS
CAST HERE

(8)
KIRJATH-
JEARIM

(4)
JERUSALEM

GILGAL

GATH (5)

(11)
BETHLEHEM

HEBRON (2)
DAVID MADE KING

(1) ZIKLAG

EDOM (13)

DAVID AND SOLOMON

tary difficulties. He fortified and garrisoned a few outposts such as Damascus, (12), Edom, (13), Hazor, (14), Megiddo, (15), and Gezer. (7). His marriage to Pharaoh's daughter secured his maritime territory and his program of preparedness brought him a reign of tranquility.

The youthful Solomon recognized his stupendous task and his first act was to seek Divine aid. He went to Gibeon where he asked God for wisdom and understanding and he got it. Then he turned his attention to building the great Temple at Jerusalem in fulfillment of the promise to David. He was assisted by King Hiram who sent great rafts of Cedars of Lebanon

(16) which he landed at Joppa (17) and loaned him architects and craftsmen. They cast their metal work in the Jordan valley (18) and the stone was taken from the quarry underneath the city.

Jeroboam of Ephraim clashed with the king toward the end of his reign but he fled to Egypt and little more was thought about it at the time. Solomon had held the territory of the kingdom of David intact, his temple was then one of the wonders of the world and his wise rule will never be forgotten. He died in 975 B.C., having reigned 40 years and was also buried on Mt. Zion by the side of his father, David. 1 Kings 2-11.

9 ISRAEL AND JUDAH
The Divided Kingdom
975–722BC
I Kings 2:2 – Kings 25

1—JERUSALEM. Rehoboam succeeded his father, Solomon, to the throne in Jerusalem without opposition. Jeroboam returned from Egypt and again urged a tax-reform which the arrogant Rehoboam flatly refused; whereupon the ten northern tribes seceded, and they were followed by Edom, Moab and Syria, leaving to Rehoboam only Judah and a fraction of Dan and Benjamin lying on the border. 1 Kings 11-12.

2—SHECHEM. The northern tribes crowned Jeroboam king at Shechem and are hereafter called the Kingdom of Israel. He fortified Shechem and Penuel (3) and established the worship of the Golden Calf at Bethel (4) and Dan (5) and his residence at Tirzah (6). Israel and Judah were divided forever. 1 Kings 12.

7—GIBETHON. After 22 years Jeroboam was succeeded by Nadab whose only act was a skirmish with the Philistines at Gilbethon. Nadab was murdered after a reign of two years and Baasha became king. During his 24 years he fortified Ramah (8) and engaged with Ben-Hadad who had pressed his boundaries to the Sea of Galilee (9). 1 Kings 15.

10—SAMARIA. Elah followed Baasha but was murdered by Zimri two years later and Zimri proclaimed himself king. Within 7 days the army crowned Omri king whereupon Zimri set Tirzah on fire and consumed himself in the flames. Omri then built Samaria, moved his capital there and a new dynasty began. 1 Kings 16.

11—SIDON. Omri arranged a marriage for his son. Ahab with Jezebel whose father, Ethbaal, was king and priest of Sidon. Ahab succeeded his father after a twelve year's reign and polluted Israel with the worship of Jezebel's Baal.

12—BROOK CHERITH. This brought Elijah the prophet to Ahab. He predicted a great drought and Ahab's threats caused him to flee to the Brook Cherith for safety. 1 Kings 17.

13—ZAREPHATH. Finally the brook dried up and Elijah found refuge with a widow at Zarephath far to the north. During this time he restored the widow's son to life. 1 Kings 17.

14—MT. CARMEL. Later Elijah and Ahab arranged a meeting on Mt. Carmel. The fire descended and consumed the prophet's sacrifice and he slew 450 prophets of Baal with his own hand. Jezebel then threatened his life and he fled again. 1 Kings 18.

15—BEERSHEBA. He first went to Beersheba where he prayed to die but was outspoken in defence of the faith. He tarried 40 days and God talked to him. 1 Kings 19.

16—DAMASCUS. God directed Elijah to go to Damascus and anoint Hazael, king of Syria, and Jehu king of Israel. He was then to go to Abel-Meholah (17) and seek out Elisha to become his own successor.

18—JEZREEL. The confiscation of Naboth's vineyard by Ahab brought the prophet to his side again and he predicted a sudden and horrible death

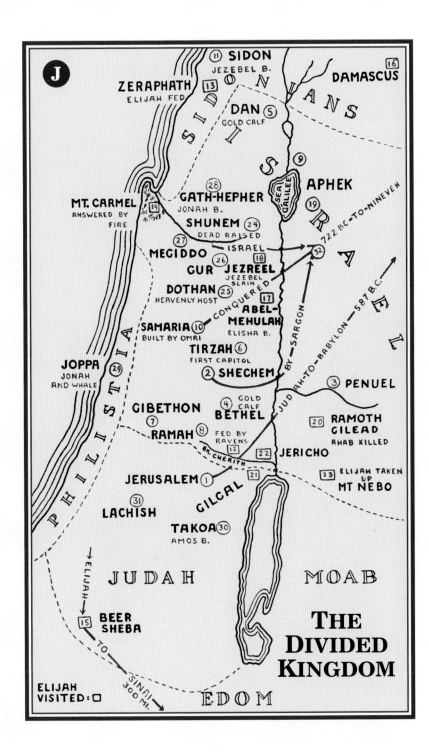

J

SIDON ⑪
JEZEBEL B.

DAMASCUS ⑯

ZERAPHATH ⑬
ELIJAH FED

DAN ⑤
GOLD CALF

SIDONIANS

GATH-HEPHER ㉘
JONAH B.

APHEK ⑨

MT. CARMEL ⑭
ANSWERED BY FIRE

SEA OF GALILEE

SHUNEM ㉔
DEAD RAISED

⑲

722 B.C.-TO-NINEVEH

MEGIDDO ㉗
ISRAEL ⑱

GUR ㉖
JEZREEL
JEZEBEL SLAIN

ISRAEL

㉜

DOTHAN ㉕
HEAVENLY HOST

CONQUERED
ABEL-MEHULAH ⑰
ELISHA B.

BY SARGON

587 B.C.

SAMARIA ⑩
BUILT BY OMRI

TIRZAH ⑥
FIRST CAPITOL

JUDAH-TO-BABYLON

JOPPA ㉙
JONAH AND WHALE

② SHECHEM

PENUEL ③

PHILISTIA

GIBETHON ⑦

④ GOLD CALF
BETHEL

RAMOTH GILEAD ⑳
AHAB KILLED

RAMAH ⑧

FED BY RAVENS

BR. CHERITH ⑫

㉒ JERICHO

JERUSALEM ①

㉑

㉓ ELIJAH TAKEN UP MT NEBO

GILGAL

LACHISH ㉛

TAKOA㉚
AMOS B.

JUDAH

MOAB

ELIJAH

BEER SHEBA ⑮

TO SINAI 300 MI.

THE DIVIDED KINGDOM

ELIJAH VISITED:▢

EDOM

29

to both the king and Jezebel.

19—APHEK. Ahab had previously defeated the Syrians at Aphek and now they met in battle at Ramouth-Gilead (20) and Ahab was pierced by an arrow. His son Ahaziah now becomes king but Elijah also predicted his death and he was succeeded by his brother, Joram. 1 Kings 22—2 Kings 1.

21—GILGAL. Elijah and Elisha then visited their schools of prophets at Gilgal and Jericho (22). Then they crossed the Jordan and went into Mt. Nebo (23) and Elijah was carried away in a chariot of fire. 2 Kings 2.

24—SHUNEM. Upon Elisha's return he healed a bitter spring at Jericho, directed the defeat of the Moabites and restored a dead boy to life at Shunem. The king gave him a residence in Samaria and soon afterward he healed Naaman of Damascus of his leprosy. 2 Kings 2-5.

25—DOTHAN. Elisha then shows his servant the army of heaven at Dothan and returns to save Samaria from a famine. 2 Kings 6-7.

26—GUR (Jenin). Upon learning of the death of Ahab, Jehu suddenly fell upon Joram and slew him; Ahazia, king of Judah (a relative who at that time was visiting Joram) was pursued to Gur and was also shot by Jehu and died at Megiddo (27). Jehu then re-turned to Jezreel and mercilessly slew Jezebel and announced himself king of Israel. This ended the Omri dynasty. 2 Kings 8-12.

Jehu destroyed Baal-worship and restored the Golden Calf but was eventually well nigh consumed by Syria. He ruled Israel 20 years and was succeeded by his son Jehoahaz (17 years) who in turn was followed by Jehoash (16 years). Elisha died two years after the death of Jehoahaz. 2 Kings 13.

28—GATH-HEPHER. Jeroboam II succeeded Jehoash and reigned 41 years, it was during this period that Jonah was born at Gath-Hepher (Nazareth) and we meet him at Joppa (29). Amos of Takoa in Judah (30) and Hosea of Israel also come under this reign. 2 Kings 13.

Then follow the last four kings in rapid succession, each one worse than his predecessor and in the ninth year of Hoshea's reign (722 B.C.) Syria, under Sargon took Samaria and carried the cream of the population to Nineveh (32) (see next map) and they were distributed to various eastern provinces. In turn Easterners were sent to Israel and intermarried with the remnant and the amalgamated race is called Samaritans to this day and for this reason hated by the Jews. 2 Kings 17.

10 EVENTS IN JUDAH
975–587BC

During this stormy period of 253 years in Israel, Judah was everything but tranquil.

1. The first king REHOBOAM introduced idolatry in Jerusalem, was attacked by Shishak of Egypt and also Jeroboam. 1 Kings 14.

2. ABIJAH failed to subjugate Israel and continued to worship "strange gods" 1 Kings 15.

3. ASA destroyed the idols, strengthened his borders and secured Ben-Hadad, Syrian King. to assist in keeping Israel under control. 1 Kings 15.

4. JEHOSHAPHAT made peace with Israel and promoted the good work his father had begun. 1 Kings 22.

5. JEHORAM put down a revolt by Edom. 2 Kings 8.

6. AHAZIA was a brother of Jehoram of Israel. His mother was Athaliah, daughter of Jezebel and promoted Baal worship in Judah. He was murdered by Jehu at Gur. Athaliah then ruled Judath for six years and was murdered.

7. JOASH was crowned at the age of 7 and the prophet was Zechariah. The country was prosperous and true worship was restored. Joash was slain by one of his own servants. 2 Kings 12.

8. AMAZIAH was a good man. he was defeated by Joash of Israel at the battle of Beth Shemish who carried away many of the treasures of Jerusalem. He was assasinated at Lachish (31) while Amos was prophet. 2 Kings 14.

9. UZIAH was the 9th king and Joel was prophet. Isaiah and Michah were prophets during (10) JOTHAM'S reign, but AHAZ (11) "spoiled the temple" sat up high places and sac-

CHRONOLOGY OF KINGS

	ISRAEL			JUDAH		
	Name	Year of Reign	Length of Reign	Name	Year of Reign	Length of Reign
975	Jeroboam I	I		{ Rehoboam	I	
	"			} "		17
	"	18		{ Abijah	I	
				} "		3
	"	20	22	Asa	I	
954	Nabad	I	}	"	2	
	"		2 }			
953	Baasha	I	}	"	3	
	"		24 }			
930	Elah	I	}	"	26	
	"		2 }			
929	Zimri		7 days }	Asa	27	
929	Omri	I	12 }	"	27	
918	Ahab	I	}	"	38	
				{ "		41
	"	4	22 }	} Jehoshaphat	I	
	"	4	}			
894	Ahaziah	I	}	"	17	
	"		2 }			
893	Jehoram	I		"	18	25
	"	5		{ Jehoram	I	
				} "		8
	"		12	{ Ahaziah		I
				}		
884	Jehu	I		{ Athaliah	I	
				} "		6
	"	7	28 }	{ Jehoash	I	
856	Jehoahaz	I	}	} "	23	
856	Jehoahaz		17 }	"	37	40
840	Joash	I	}			
	"	2	16 }	{ Amaziah	I	
825	Jeroboam II	I	}	} "	15	
	"	27	41 }	{ "		29
				} Uzziah (Azariah)	I	
773	Zecharia		6 mo. }	" "	38	
772	Shallum		1 mo. }			
772	Menahem	I	}	" "	39	
	"		10 }			
761	Pekahiah	I	}	" "	50	
	"		2 }			
759	Pekah	I	}	" "	52	
	"	2	}	" " "		52
	"	17	20 J	{ Jotham	I	
				{ "		16
				{ Ahaz	I	
730	Hoshea	I	}	"	12	
	"	3	}	{ "		16
				} Hezekiah	1	
722	(Samaria taken)		9	"	6	

31

rified his own sons to Moloch. He suffered at the hands of the Syrians, Edomites and Philistines. Isaiah and Michah are the prophets.

12—HEZEKIAH crushed Baal worship, was bankrupt by the invasion of Sennacherib but finally enjoyed peace and prosperity while Nahum was prophet. 2 Kings 15-20.

13. MANASSEH was hard-hearted and ungodly, but he paid and later repented. 2 Kings 21 and Ch. 33.

14. AMON was no better and was slain by his servants in his own house. 2 Kings 21.

15. JOSIAH discovered the lost book of the Law and had it read to the people. He died in battle at Megiddo (27). The prophets were Jeremiah and Zephaniah. 2 Kings 22, 23.

16. JEHOAHAZ reigned but three months when he was dethroned by the King of Egypt who took him to his own country where he died. Egypt then appointed Eliakim King of Judah and changed his name to Jehoiakim. 2 Kings 23.

17. ELIAKIN (Jehoakim) was made a servant to Babylon after eleven year's reign and was succeeded by

18. JEHOAKIN who was taken prisoner to Babylon 3 months later together with "many mighty of the land" and Zedakiah (Mattaniah) was appointed by Babylon in his stead. Jerusalem was taken during his reign and he together with all the finest people of the land were carried away by Nebuchadnezzar. The prophets were Jeremiah, Habakkuk and Obeliah, but Jeremiah was permitted to remain with the remnant in Judah. 2 Kings 24-25. 587 B.C.

11 CHRONOLOGY OF KINGS
Israel in Assyria – Judah in Babylon
729–400BC

Daniel, Ezekiel, Ezra, Nehemiah, Esther

Babylon was conquered by Nineveh at the hands of Tiglath-Pileser in 729 B.C. His successor, Shalmaneser began the siege of Samaria but died before it capitulated and Sargon his successor, is credited for its overthrow. He carried all the better class to Nineveh in 722 B.C. and from there they were sent in smaller groups to various parts of his domains where they eventually lost their identity and never returned.

Upon the other hand many were sent from these same parts to colonize the territory vacated by Israel. These intermarried with the remnant which had been left in Israel and the new race was called Samaritans. The same thing must have occurred in the East and the identity of the "ten tribes" was entirely lost.

Nebo-Polasser the Babylonian defeated and destroyed Nineveh in 607 B.C. and Nebuchadnezzar his son founded the New Babylonian Empire two years later. He also laid Jerusalem in ruins and destroyed the temple in 587 B.C., carried the king. Zedekiah, all "desirables" and everything that had value to Babylon. Only Jeremiah was given a choice to go or stay and he remained with the undesirables left in Judah. Both Daniel and Ezekiel are in Babylon.

Gadaliah was appointed governor by Nebuchadnezzar but was slain by a discouraged group of the remnant who fled to Egypt, and they compelled Jeremiah to accompany them and not a trace of their whereabouts was ever found.

In Babylon, many of the Jews were highly esteemed. Daniel and others were appointed to high office, many went into business and when they were permitted to return to Jerusalem, the majority preferred to remain in the East but made large contributions toward the rehabilitation of their native land.

Cyrus the Medo-Persian king took Babylon in 538 B.C.; two years later he released all Jews who wished to return to Jerusalem and appointed Zerubbabel governor of Judea who rebuilt the temple which was named for him in 515 B.C.

Esther was made queen through her marriage to Xerxes in 478 B.C. and resided in the palace at Shushan (Susa) which was the capital.

Artaxerxes sent Ezra to Jerusalem in 458 B.C. Then in 445 he sent Nehemiah to rebuild the Holy City who returned to Persia in 434. Two years later he was sent back to Jerusalem with papers of authority and a contribution from the king to see that the work was being done correctly and to complete it.

While Nehemiah was building walls Ezra was building character among the people and when the work was finished they held a great dedication ceremony. Ezra read the law to the throng who responded with "Amen!" and they bowed their heads and worshipped the Lord with their faces to the ground. "After many days" the people dispersed and a new era began in Judea. Malachi followed as prophet and wrote his book about the year 400 B.C.

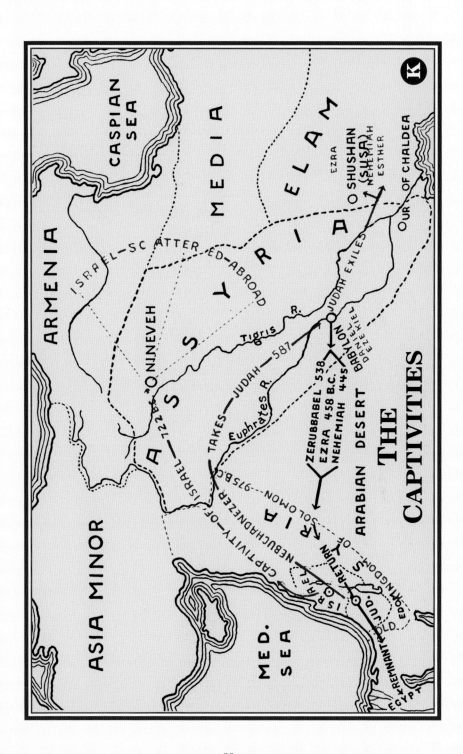

CASPIAN SEA

ARMENIA

ASIA MINOR

MED. SEA

MEDIA

ELAM

SYRIA

ARABIAN DESERT

ISRAEL-SCATTERED-ABROAD

NINEVEH

Tigris R.

Euphrates R.

ISRAEL—722 B.C.

TAKES—JUDAH—587

CAPTIVITY-OF-ISRAEL

NEBUCHADNEZZER

KINGDOMS OF SOLOMON—975 B.C.

RETURN OF ISRAEL

ISRAEL

JUDAH

OLD EDOM

REMNANT

EGYPT

JUDAH EXILES

BABYLON

DANIEL

EZEKIEL

ZERUBBABEL 538

EZRA 458 B.C.

NEHEMIAH 445

EZRA

SHUSHAN (SUSA)

NEHEMIAH

ESTHER

UR OF CHALDEA

THE CAPTIVITIES

33

12 MALACHI TO JESUS

The hand of Persia continued to be upon Palestine until 330 B.C. when Babylon fell under the pressure of Alexander the Great and Palestine was included as a part of his victory. But Alexander died in Babylon seven years later (323 B.C.) and leaving no legitimate heir, his great conquests were seized by generals who had been associated with him.

After ten year's rivalry among them, Syria and Egypt became independent kingdoms, and Palestine lying between them, became not only their battle ground, but was alternately subject to each until the day of Judas Maccabaeus (165 B.C.) who led the Jews into a successful revolution.

The Maccabaean reign of 100 years was a turbulent one at best and the end came quickly when internal difficulties arose between Hyrcanus II and his brother, Aristobulus II. regarding their successorship to the throne. Pompey of Rome was called upon to settle the dispute (63 B.C.) and soon took advantage of his opportunity to annex the country to his own domain.

The Sadducees and Pharisees are first mentioned in history about the year 109 B.C. But by 63 B.C. they had gained much power and were bitter enemies. And this incident of division in the Maccabaean family is said to have been due to their meddling in the political affairs of their country. We will also find that their antagonism to Jesus sent Him to the Cross; not through any evidence that they produced, but because of their influence upon the people.

Through the support of Antony, Herod the Great, an Idumean, captured Jerusalem (37 A.D.) and assumed the title of King of the Jews. He married Mariamne, the last of the Maccabaean family, but murdered her (29 B.C.) and later had their three sons put to death. This Herod met the Wise Men from the East (5 B.C.) and slew the babies of Bethlehem in his fear that Jesus might supplant him as King. He died in Jericho of a loathsome disease (4 B.C.) and the child Jesus was brought back from Egypt.

Herod's Kingdom, which was all Palestine, (see map) was divided among his three sons. Judea and Samaria to Archelaus; Galilee and Perea to Antipas, and north-east Palestine to Philip.

ARCHELAUS was deposed by Rome in 6 A.D. and afterward Judea and Samaria were made a Roman Province and the fifth Procurator was Pontius Pilate who held office when Jesus was crucified.

ANTIPAS beheaded John the Baptist, participated in the trial of Jesus and was exiled by Rome in 40 A.D.

AUGUSTUS was Emperor of Rome 31 B.C.-14 A.D.

TIBERIUS, 14 A.D.-37 A.D.

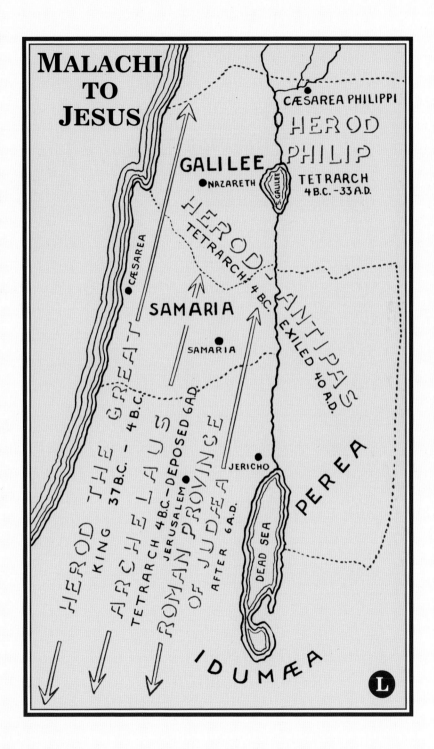

MALACHI
TO
JESUS

CÆSAREA PHILIPPI

HEROD PHILIP
TETRARCH
4 B.C. - 33 A.D.

GALILEE
● NAZARETH

S. GALILEE

HEROD ANTIPAS
TETRARCH 4 B.C.
EXILED 40 A.D.

● CÆSAREA

SAMARIA
● SAMARIA

PEREA

● JERICHO

DEAD SEA

HEROD THE GREAT
KING 37 B.C. - 4 B.C.

ARCHELAUS
TETRARCH 4 B.C. - DEPOSED 6 A.D.

JERUSALEM ●

ROMAN PROVINCE OF JUDÆA
AFTER 6 A.D.

IDUMÆA

L

35

IV The New Testament: The Ministry of Jesus Christ (1)

Zacharius and the angel. Page 38

Mary shares her news with Elizabeth. Page 38 §1

No room at the inn. Page 38 §2

Three Wise Men from the East follow the star. Page 38 §3

The three Wise Men present their gifts. Page 38 §3

The massacre of the innocents. Page 38 §4

Jesus in the Wilderness. Page 40 §3

Jesus calls Peter and Andrew. Page 40 §3

Water into wine at Cana. Page 40 §5

The child in the manger. Page 38 §2

Shepherds come to worship Jesus. Page 38 §2

Simeon encounters the infant Jesus in the Temple. Page 38 §3

The Holy Family flees Herod for Egypt. Page 38 §4

The boy Jesus in the Temple, talking with the priests. Page 38 §6

John baptizes Jesus. Page 40 §1

Jesus and Nicomedus. Page 40 §7

The great catch of fish. Page 42 §3

The sick man set down through the roof. Page 42 §4

At the well of Bethesda. Page 42 §5

13 JESUS' FIRST THIRTY YEARS
5BC – AD25

	MATT.	MARK	LUKE	JOHN
The announcement of the birth of John was made to Zacharias while officiating in the temple at Jerusalem.			1:5-25	
Six months later the announcement of the birth of Jesus was made to Mary at Nazareth.			1:26-38	
Announcement of Jesus' birth to Joseph, Nazareth.	1:18-25			
1—AIN KAIRIM. Mary visits Elizabeth at Ain Kairim (?) (tradition).			1:39-56	
Mary returns home and John the Baptist is born.			1:57-80	
2—BETHLEHEM. Mary and Joseph go to Bethlehem to register and Jesus is born there.			2:1-7	
Angels announce Jesus' birth to shepherds in a near-by field who immediately come to Bethlehem seeking him.			2:8-20	
Jesus circumcised at Bethlehem when eight days old.			2:21	
3—JERUSALEM. After 40 days Jesus is taken to Jerusalem where he is dedicated and is seen by Simeon and Anna who have been waiting for his advent, and returns to Bethlehem.			2:22-39	
Wise men from the East come seeking him after they had seen his star in the East and they first encountered King Herod in Jerusalem. He sent them to Bethlehem where they made their offerings and returned to their own country by another route.	2:1-12			
4—EGYPT. The infuriated king murdered all the male children in Bethlehem in an effort to destroy his supposed rival and Jesus was taken to Egypt.	2:13-18			
5—NAZARETH. Herod died within a year and sometime later the Holy Family returned to Nazareth.	2:19-23			
(Archelaus was deposed A.D. 6 when Jesus was 11 and Judea was ruled by procurators after that)				
6—JERUSALEM. Jesus was reared in Nazareth until he was thirty. At the age of 12 (7 A.D.) he was taken to Jerusalem, consulted the Doctors, was lost from his parents but returned to Nazareth and was in silence until his baptism. (Summer A.D. 26)			2:40-52	
(Augustus was succeeded by Tiberius A.D. 14)				

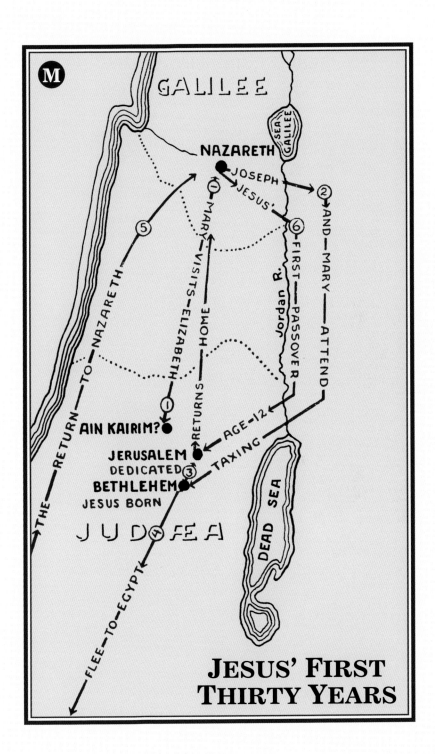

JESUS' FIRST THIRTY YEARS

14 JESUS BEGINS MINISTRY
Summer AD25 – December AD26

	MATT.	MARK	LUKE	JOHN
1—NAZARETH.— John comes announcing the Messiah and baptizing the people in the Jordan. (2) Jesus visits him there and is baptized also. (Summer A.D. 26)	3:1-17	1:1-11	3:1-23	
3—MT. QUARANTINIA. Immediately following his baptism Jesus was led into the wilderness where he fasted for 40 days and was tempted. A mountain in full view of the Jordan, 10 miles west is the traditional "wilderness."	4:1-11	1:12-13	4:1-13	
When Jesus returns, John is at Bethbara east of Jordan (4): he is stating the mission of both himself and Jesus to whom he refers as "The Lamb of God." Two men follow and tarry with Jesus over night. One was Andrew who introduces his brother, Peter to him next morning.				1:19-34
				1:35-42
5—CANA. Philip was the other and introduces Nathaniel of Cana and they all journey to that city together next morning..				1:43-51
Jesus' mother is in Cana attending a wedding when they arrive and he is invited and performs his first miracle. (Changes water to wine)				2:1-11
6—CAPERNAUM. Accompanied by his mother and brothers, Jesus goes to Capernaum with the other three and spends a few days when he departs for the Passover in Jerusalem, Apr. 11, A.D. 27.				2:12
7—JERUSALEM. Upon his first visit to Jerusalem, Jesus accused the "Money-changers" with making his Father's House a den of thieves and drove them out.				2:13-22
During the feast Nicodemus, a teacher of the Jews, called on him by night and Jesus discoursed with him on the New Birth.				2:23-3:21
After the feast Jesus continued to teach and baptize in various parts of Judea. At this time John was at Aenon and corrected errors the people held regarding Jesus' mission.				3:22-36
8—SYCHAR. Leaving Judea, Jesus proceeded due north to Jacob's well (Samaria)				
At Jacob's well Jesus discussed the "Water of Life" to a Samaritan woman who said she expected the Messiah and he admitted that the Messiah was speaking to her at that time.				4:4-26
Jesus and his disciples tarried two days in Sychar (Samaria) two miles from the well and many believed his teaching. Then he moved on north into Galilee and came to Cana (5) again.				4:27-42

40

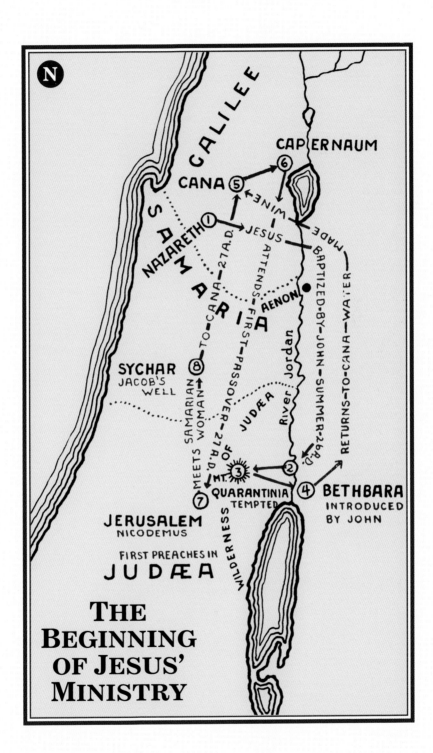

THE
BEGINNING
OF JESUS'
MINISTRY

15 BEGINNING OF JESUS' MINISTRY IN GALILEE
December AD26 – Summer AD27

	MATT.	MARK	LUKE	JOHN
1—SYCHAR. When Jesus arrived in Cana (2) from Sychar a Nobleman (King's Officer) from Capernaum was waiting for him to come and heal his son. Though the boy was 20 miles away he spoke the word and the boy was healed—the first cure by Jesus.				4:46-54
3—NAZARETH. Jesus now sends his disciples to Capernaum and he goes to Nazareth 5 miles west. He is called upon to speak in the synogogue but his teaching is rejected and they try to take his life and he escapes to Capernaum. (4)	4:13-16		4:16-31	
One day while walking by the seashore he called Andrew, Peter, James and John to follow him. He then taught a multitude from a boat and the miraculous catch of fishes followed.	4:18-22	1:16-20	5:1-11	
The following Sabbath they all attended the synagogue in Capernaum and he taught the people. When the sermon ended Jesus healed a desperate demoniac. He then went home with Peter and healed his mother-in-law and that evening he healed multitudes of sick on the streets of the city.	8:14-17	1:21-34	4:31-41	
4—GALILEAN TOUR. Jesus slipped away that night and was found next day in a desert but refused to return. Instead he made a short tour of Galilee north of Capernaum. at which time he healed one leper.	4:23	1:35-45	4:42-44	
4—CAPERNAUM. Upon his return from the Galilean tour he was preaching in a house in Capernaum when a man was let down through the roof before him and Jesus forgave the man's sins and healed him in the presence of a group of criticising Pharisees.	9:2-8	2:1-12	5:17-26	
Later Jesus called Matthew a Publican (Tax-collector) to follow him.	9:9-13	2:13-17	5:27-32	
Then he discusses fasting with the disciples of John.	9:14-17	2:18-22	5:33-39	
5—JERUSALEM. Jesus now goes to Jerusalem to attend a feast (not a Passover) and he heals a man at the Pool of Bethesda who has been paralyzed for 38 years. Later the man is questioned and Jesus defends him in a great address.				Chap. 5
Journeying back towards Capernaum, the Pharisees who were following Jesus criticised him for plucking grain on the Sabbath, but he justified it.	12:1-8	2:23-28	6:1-5	
Returning to Capernaum (4) Jesus attends the synagogue service and heals a man of a withered hand on the Sabbath and is condemned by Pharisees.	12:9-14	3:1-6	6:6-11	

42 .

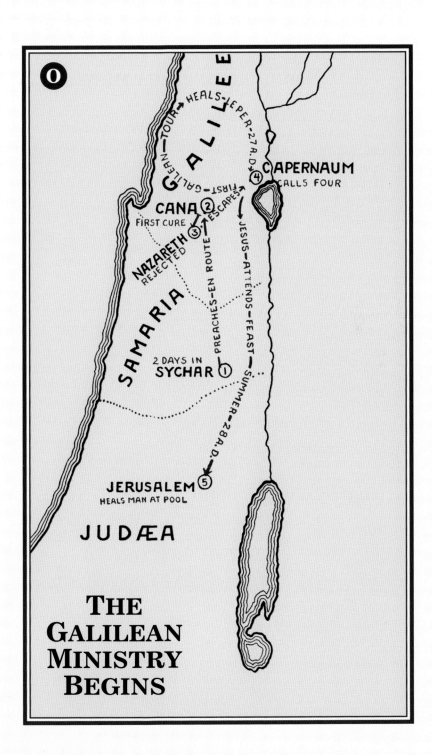

GALILEE

HEALS LEPER 27 A.D.

GALILEAN TOUR

FIRST GALILEAN

CAPERNAUM
CALLS FOUR

CANA
FIRST CURE

NAZARETH
REJECTED

ESCAPES

JESUS ATTENDS FEAST

SAMARIA

PREACHES EN ROUTE

SUMMER 28 A.D.

2 DAYS IN
SYCHAR

JERUSALEM
HEALS MAN AT POOL

JUDÆA

THE GALILEAN MINISTRY BEGINS

V The New Testament: The Ministry of Jesus Christ (2)

The Sermon on the Mount. Page 46 §3

Jesus calms the storm. Page 46 §8

Feeding the 5,000. Page 46 §13

The parable of the Good Samaritan. Page 50 §1

The parable of the Lost Sheep. Page 50 §4

Jesus teaches the Lord's Prayer. Page 50 §3

Jesus' triumphal entry to Jerusalem. Page 52 §2

Clearing the Temple of the moneychangers. Page 52

The Last Supper. Page 52

Jesus walks upon the waters Page 46 §14

The Transfiguration.
Page 48 §6

The Feast of the Tabernacles. Page 48 §9

The parable of the Prodigal Son.
Page 50 §4

The raising of Lazarus.
Page 50 §5

Zacchaeus in the tree.
Page 52 §8

Jesus before Pilate.
Page 52

The crucifixion.
Page 52

Jesus entombed. Page 52

16 SECOND STAGE OF THE GALILEAN MINISTRY Summer AD27 – Passover, 18 April AD28

	MATT.	MARK	LUKE	JOHN
1—CAPERNAUM. By this time the fame of Jesus had spread far and wide and people from every corner of the country came to see him and many believed.	4:23-25	3:7-12	6:17-19	
2—GENNESARET. Jesus selected 12 men from the great crowd and ascended from the plain of Gennesaret to Mt. Hattan (3) and gave the Beatitudes and delivered the Sermon on the Mount.	5, 6, 7	3:13-19	6:12-49	
4—CAPERNAUM. The Multitudes follow him from the Mount to Capernaum where a centurion is waiting for him to heal his servant who is at the point of death.	8:5-13		7:1-10	
From Capernaum Jesus goes to Nain (5) 20 miles south where he restores life to the son of a widow and returns (6) immediately.			7:11-17	
Upon his return from Nain to Capernaum he receives his last mesage from John the Baptist who inquires whether he is "The Messiah."	11:2-30		7:18-35	
He now dines with Simon a Pharisee, is anointed by a woman and is criticized for permitting it.			7:36-50	
7—SECOND TOUR OF GALILEE. Then follows his second tour of Galilee and he is accompanied by women.			8:1-3	
When he returned to Capernaum he warned the Pharisees of an "Eternal Sin" and explained what true kinship is.	12:22-50	3:19-35	8:19-21	
8—BY THE SEA. Here his sea-side parables are delivered from a boat.	13:1-53	4:1-34	8:4-18	
He raises anchor and sails across the sea to Gadara and calms a storm enroute (9)	8:23-27	4:35-41	8:22-25	
10—GADARA. At Gadara on the east side Jesus heals two terrible maniacs.	8:28-34	5:1-20	8:26-39	
Jesus had been away only one day, but when he returned to Capernaum (1) Jarius the ruler of the Synagogue, was waiting for him to heal his daughter. She died in the meantime and he restored her to life. He also healed a woman who had had an issue of blood for 12 years.	9:18-26	5:21-43	8:40-56	
Two blind men and a dumb demoniac were waiting outside Jarius' house and were also healed.	9:27-34			
11—NAZARETH. Jesus now makes another visit to Nazarath where he is rejected the second time. Then he makes the third tour of Galilee (12) and sends out the disciples to preach and heal the sick.	9:35-11:1	6:1-29	9:1-9	
He returns to Capernaum, crosses the sea and feeds 5000 (13) and that night he calms the storm while walking on the water (14).	14:13-36	6:30-56	9:10-17	6:1-21
Next day he discoursed on "The Bread of Life", (2) the crowd could not receive it and dispersed.				6:22-71

46

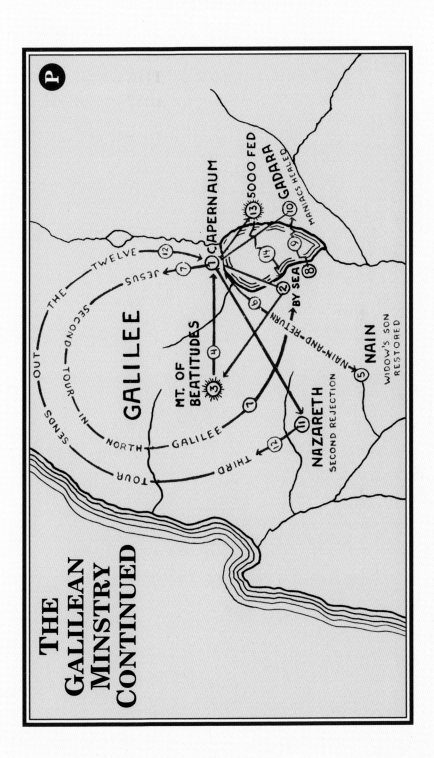

47

CLOSING DAYS OF JESUS' MINISTRY
April AD28 – November AD29

	MATT.	MARK	LUKE	JOHN
1—TYRE AND SIDON COUNTRY. Jesus probably did not attend the Passover which was in session about this time, but from Capernaum he turned north to the region about Tyre and Sidon and only one cure was effected—the Syrophoenician girl.	15:21-28	7:24-30		
2—DECAPOLIS. Upon his return he avoided Capernaum and came through Decapolis. He healed a deaf man and multitudes of others and fed 4000 as he had fed 5000 before.	15:29-38	7:31-8:1-9		
3—MAGDALA. Then he crossed the sea to Magdala where the Pharisees and Sadducees demanded a sign which he refused to give.	15:39-16:12	8:10-21		
4—BETHSAIDA-JULIUS. Jesus again avoiding Capernaum, immediately crossed the sea to Bethsaida-Julius and healed a blind man, the first he ever treated more than once.		8:22-26		
5—CAESAREA PHILIPPI. Jesus and the disciples now turn north to Caesarea-Philippi where Peter confesses Christ's Deity and Jesus foretells his own death and resurrection.	16:13-28	8:1-27-9:1		
6—MT. HERMON. From here Jesus takes James, Peter and John into the mountain and is transfigured. They meet Moses and Elijah and God speaks to them.	17:1-13	9:2-13	9:28-36	
7—HEALS BOY. Returning to the base of the mountain they found the remaining 9 disciples trying to heal a demented boy. Jesus healed him and then criticised their lack of faith.	17:14-20	9:14-29	9:37-43	
He again foretells his death and resurrection.	17:22, 23	9:30-32	9:43-45	
8—CAPERNAUM. They all return from here to Capernaum (probably only over night) and the coin is found in the fishe's mouth.	17:24-27			
That same night Jesus also gave the disciples a great discourse on humility and forgiveness and demanded that they become as little children.	Ch.18-19: 33-50	9:46-50		
9—JERUSALEM. Next morning they all leave Capernaum for Jerusalem (November 29 A.D.) to attend the Feast of Tabernacles and the authorities there confront Jesus with the woman taken in sin. He then discourses with them on the Light of the World and Spiritual Freedom.				7:1-8:59

48

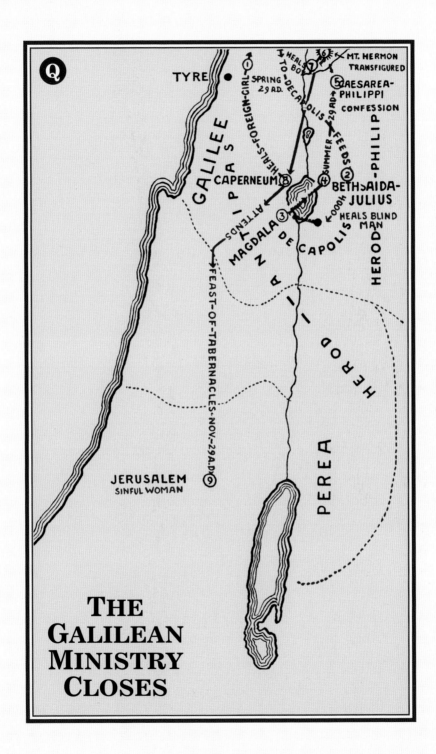

THE GALILEAN MINISTRY CLOSES

18

JESUS' MINISTRY IN PEREA
November AD29 – Sunday before
Passover, AD30

	MATT.	MARK	LUKE	JOHN
1—TOUR PEREA. Leaving Jerusalem Jesus turned northward through Samaria but was not well received. He then crosed the Jordan into Perea, told the story of the "Good Samaritan" and sent out the 70 to prepare the way for his future visit.			9:51-10:37	
2—BETHANY. He then made a visit to Martha, Mary and Lazarus at Bethany.			10:38-42	
3—POOL SILOAM. (Page 42) During this visit he healed a man who had been born blind, directing him to wash in the pool of Siloam. Then he defended the man when he was being accosted by the officers of the temple. He told them of the Good Shepherd, Abundant life and refused to answer their catch questions.				Ch. 9-10:21
MT. OLIVES. Jesus teaches his disciples how to pray. (Lord's Prayer)			11:1-13	
TEMPLE COURT. Directs great discourses against the Pharisees and his teaching on trust in God, and the judgement, are lightly received.			11:14, Ch. 12	
4—PEREA (2nd Tour) Great crowds greeted him there and his first act was to heal a woman on a Sabbath. He said, "Few are Saved", and was not fearful when they threatened him with Herod.			13:10-35	
Jesus dined with a Pharisee, healed a man who had dropsy and was criticised.			14:1-24	
This was followed by the parables of the "Lost sheep", and the "Lost Coin" and the "Prodigal son".			Ch. 15	
Parable on "Stewardship" and the "Rich man and Lazarus", followed.			Ch. 16	
5—TO BETHANY. At this juncture Jesus was interrupted by messengers from Bethany, saying, Lazarus was seriously ill. When he arrived, Lazarus had been dead four days but he restored him to life and many believed.				11:1-46
6—EPHRAIM. But it only increased the antagonism of the leaders of the Jerusalem Jews who threatened his life and Jesus retired to Ephraim for a few days after which he moved north (Jenin?) where he cleansed the Ten Lepers.			17:11-19	11:47-54
7—PEREA. (3rd Tour) From here he went back to Perea. He discussed the coming kingdom and the prayer of the Pharisee and Publican, but only a few heard him this time.			17:20-18:14	
The crowds had forsaken him, except a few women, and he blessed their children.	19:13-18	10:13-16	18:15-17	

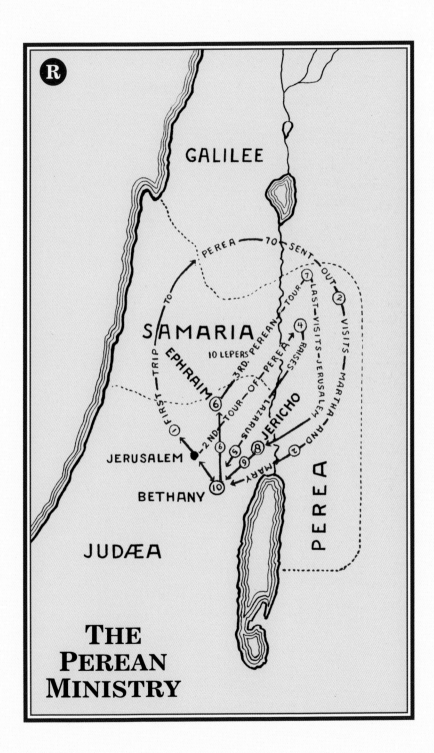

R

GALILEE

PEREA — TO — SENT

TO

SAMARIA

EPHRAIM

10 LEPERS

3RD — PEREAN — TOUR — OF — PEREA

LAST — VISITS — JERUSALEM

VISITS — MARTHA — AND

FIRST — TRIP

2ND — TOUR — OF — PEREA

RAISES — LAZARUS — AND — MARY

JERICHO

JERUSALEM

BETHANY

JUDÆA

PEREA

THE PEREAN MINISTRY

	MATT.	MARK	LUKE	JOHN

Jesus's last act in Perea was his interview with the Rich young Ruler who turned away sorrowfuly.

8—JERICHO. Jesus now proceeds on his final trip to Jerusalem and just as he was approaching Jericho he healed the Blind men—one was Bartimeas. He dined with Zacchaeus the publican in Jericho, and was criticised.

9—Then as he crossed the desert he gave the parable of the Pounds.

10—BETHANY. When he arrived in Bethany. Simon the leper whom Jesus had healed, made a great supper in his honor and Mary annointed him. (Fri. March 31)

	MATT.	MARK	LUKE	JOHN
	19:16-20:16	10:17-31	18:18-30	
	20:29-34	10:46-52	18:35-43	
			19:1-10	
			19:11-28	
	26:6-13	14:3-9	11:55-12:11	

19 PASSION WEEK
Sunday 2 April – Sunday 9 April AD30

Jesus spent Friday night and Saturday (the Sabbath) in Bethany (1).

2—SUNDAY. He made his Triumphal entry into Jerusalem.

MONDAY enroute to the Holy City he cursed the barren fig tree, and again drove the money changers from the temple.

TUESDAY as soon as he reached the the temple the leaders challenged Jesus' authority. He gave them three parables of warning. whereupon they return three questions. Jesus then gives them the unanswerable question regarding David and then pronounces "woes" against the leaders.

He compliments the widow's two mites. Gentiles seek Jesus and Jews reject him.

He predicts the destruction of Jerusalem and the end of the world.

Judas is bribed to betray Jesus.

(Jesus retired to Bethany each evening but there is no record of **WEDNESDAY**).

THURSDAY, all day he spent in Bethany. He sent two disciples to the Holy City who procured an Upper Room (3) for the Passover feast. Jesus came over late in the evening, participated in the Paschal meal and then instituted the Lord's supper. Judas leaves during the Meal.

Then follows Jesus' farewell address. The intercessory prayer, a hymn then they went out. (3 to 4)

FRIDAY (after midnight) Agony in the Garden of Gethsemane. (4)

Betrayal and arrest. (4 to 5)

Trial before Annas (6) Caiaphas (7) the Sanhedrin (8).

Trial before Pilate ; (9) Herod; (10) and the second time before Pilate.

The crucifixion and burial. (11)

SATURDAY all day in the tomb; the watch.

	MATT.	MARK	LUKE	JOHN
	21:1-11	11:1-11	19:29-44	12:12-19
	21:12-17	11:12-19	19:45-48	
	21:23-Ch. 23	11:27 12:40	Ch. 20	
		12:41-44	21:1-4	12:20-50
	Ch. 24-25 26:1-16	Ch. 13 14:10-11	21:5-38 22:1-6	
	26:17-30 26:31-35	14:12-26 14:27-31	22:7-30 22:31-38	13:1-30 13:31-16:23
				Ch. 17
	26:36-46	14:32-42	22:39-46	18:1
	26:47-56	14:43-52	22:47-53	18:1-11
	26:57-27:10	14:53-72	22:54-71	18:12-27
	27:11-31	15:1-20	23:1-25	18:38-19:16
	27:32-61	15:21-47	23:26-56	19:16-42
	27:62-66			

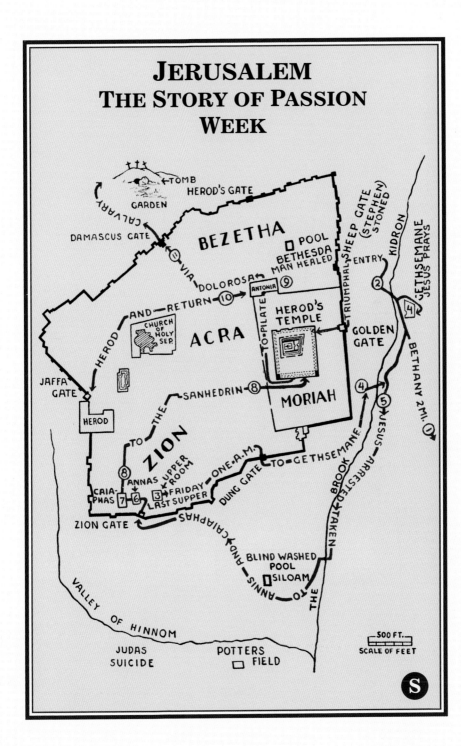

VI The New Testament: Spreading the Word: the Acts of the Apostles

The risen Christ. Page 56.

Christ appears on the road to Emmaus. Page 56 §1

Saul looks on at the martyrdom of Stephen. Page 56

Christ appears to Thomas and the disciples. Page 56 §1

Philip and the Ethiopian. Page 56

Paul before Felix. Page 64 §1

Paul before Herod Agrippa. Page 64 §3

Paul's ship caught in the storm off Malta. Page 64 §6ff

The conversion of Saul on the road to Damascus. Page 56

The Ascension.
Page 56 §4

The disciples filled with the
Holy Spirit. Page 56

Peter and John heal a cripple
at the Gate Beautiful. Page 56

Saul's escape from
Damascus. Page 56

Paul in Corinth. Page 60 §15

Paul: the 'Man of
Macedonia'. Page 60 §6

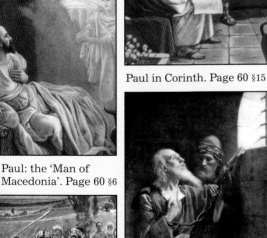

Paul arrested in Jerusalem. Page 62 §15

Paul in prison: 'I have fought
a good fight'. Page 64

Paul marched along the
Appian Way to Rome.
Page 64 §12

The martyrdom of St Paul. Page 64

20 EVENTS AFTER THE RESURRECTION
Sunday 9 April AD30 – AD37

	MATT.	MARK	LUKE	JOHN
The resurrection early Sunday morning. (Page 52).	28:1-10	16:1-11	24:12	20:1-18
1—EMMAUS. Appearance to the men of Emmaus. (Sunday evening)		16-12-13	24:13-25	
Appearance to the disciples at Jerusalem, upper room (Page 52) (Sunday night).				
Second appearance to the disciples (Apr. 16) upper room.		16:14	24:36-43	
				20:26-29
2—BY SEA. Appearance to 7 by the Sea of Galilee.				21:1-24
3—IN MOUNTAIN. Appearance to the eleven on a mountain in Galilee.	28:16-20	16:15-18		
4—OLIVET. Final appearance and the ascension from Olivet near Bethany, Thursday, May 18, 30 A.D.		16:19-20	24:44-53	

UPPER ROOM. Ten days later (May 28) on the day of Pentecost, the disciples who had been waiting in the Upper room (Page 52) for the fulfillment of Jesus' promise were filled with the Holy Spirit; Peter preached and 3000 converts were made. Acts ch. 1 & 2.

There were visitors here from many countries who heard them speak in their own language. and became converts. These formed the nucleus of a church in these various countries when evangelists arrived later to declare the gospel of Christ. For the far-flung effect of this great event see the next map. Acts. 2:8-11.

Peter and John heal a cripple at the Gate, Beautiful. (See Temple 1) Acts 3:1-10.

This incident aroused the authorities who arrested the apostles at Solomons porch (Temple 2) and cast them in prison over night. A hearing was given them next day (Temple 3) and they preached to their persecutors and many believed. Acts. 3, 4.

The disciples held all things in common, their number multiplied even though they were constantly persecuted. They, no doubt continued to reside on Zion. Acts 5, 6.

Stephen was stoned to death near the gate which now bears his name at the hands of Saul of Tarsus for his outspoken defense of the faith. (Map S) 32 A.D. Acts. 7.

Then followed a merciless persecution of the church and all the Christians, except the apostles, fled in every direction preaching the word. We have a record of but one, Philip, who went to Samaria (5) and made many converts. From there he went down toward Gaza (6) and baptized the Ethiopian Eunuch: next to Azotus (Ashdod) (7) and thence to Caesarea his home. Acts 8.

In the meantime Saul went to Damascus (9) to seize the Christians there, but as he neared the city he was converted and preached the gospel in the church he had come to destroy. Acts 9:1-22.

He immediately isolated himself in the Arabian desert (10) where he remained 3 years. Gal. 1:17.

Then he returned to Damascus (11) and his preaching so infuriated the Jews that he was compelled to flee by night (12) and he came to Jerusalem where he tarried 15 days. Acts 9:23-26.

He aroused the smouldering enmity of the Jews at Jerusalem but he escaped to Caesarea, again by night, and from thence to Tarsus (13), his original home. A.D. 35. (For Tarsus see page 58). Acts 9:26-30.

14—LYDDA. In a preaching tour now made by Peter. he healed Aeneas at Lydda. Acts 9:32-36.

15—JOPPA. From there he was called to Joppa and raised Dorcas to life. Acts 0:36-43.

Because of a vision he saw at Joppa he was led to Caesarea (8) where Cornelius, the first Gentile convert was made and then he returned to Jerusalem.

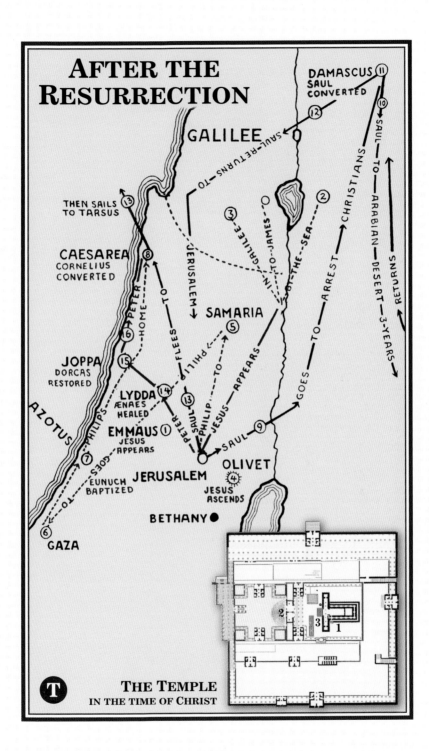

AFTER THE RESURRECTION

GALILEE

DAMASCUS
SAUL CONVERTED ⑪

⑫

SAUL-RETURNS-TO ⑩

SAUL TO ARABIAN DESERT—3·YEARS

RETURNS

TO ARREST CHRISTIANS

THEN SAILS TO TARSUS ⑬

CAESAREA
CORNELIUS CONVERTED

⑧

③

IN GALILEE

TO JAMES

OF·THE·SEA ②

JERUSALEM↓

SAMARIA
⑤

PETER HOME

⑯

JOPPA
DORCAS RESTORED

⑮

PETER FLEES TO

PHILIP TO

JESUS APPEARS

GOES TO ARREST

AZOTUS

LYDDA
ÆNAES HEALED

⑭

⑬

SAUL

PHILIP

EMMAUS ①
JESUS APPEARS

PETER

SAUL ⑨

PHILIPS

GOES TO

OLIVET
④
JESUS ASCENDS

⑦

EUNUCH BAPTIZED

JERUSALEM

BETHANY ●

⑥

GAZA

THE TEMPLE
IN THE TIME OF CHRIST

2   3   1

21 PAUL'S FIRST MISSIONARY JOURNEY
AD43 – AD49

Note: The emperor Tiberius was succeeded by Caligula in 37 A.D. and he by Claudius in 41 at which time Herod Agrippa I is appointed king of Judaea and Samaria. Herod died 3 years later (44 A.D.) and Claudius appointed Cuspius Fadus, procurator.

2—ANTIOCH. Barnabas is sent from Jerusalem to the newly organized Gentile church at Antioch. Acts 11:19-24.

3—TARSUS. Barnabas goes to Tarsus and brings Saul back to Antioch (4) A.D. 43 and they work there together for more than a year. Acts 11:25-27.

In 45 A.D. Saul and Barnabas take an offering to the Jerusalem church to relieve a famine. (Route 2). Acts 11:27-30.

(Note: Tiberius Alexander succeeds Fadus as procurator A.D. 46)

ACTS 13

Saul and Barnabas continued their work at Antioch and the church sets them apart as missionaries in A.D. 47.

5—SELUCIA. So these two, accompanied by John Mark, start on the first missionary tour ever made to a foreign country. They follow the Orontes about ten miles to its mouth, to Seleucia.

6—SALAMIS. From Seleucia, they sailed to Salamis on the Island of Cyprus and preached in the synagogue.

7—PAPHOS. From Salamis they moved westward across the Island to Paphos, the capitol, where Sergius Paulus, the Governor, was converted. Elymas, a sorceror at this place was stricken with blindess and Saul's name was changed to Paul.

8—PERGA. The trio sailed from Pa-phos northward to Perga in Pamphylia where Mark, for some reason, left the company and returned to Jerusalem.

9—ANTIOCH. Barnabas and Paul now moved northward to Antioch in Pisidia and preached in the synagogue two Sabbaths, but they were driven out of the city by the Jewish leaders and moved on to Iconium (10) where they met with the same Jewish hostility.

ACTS 14

11—LYSTRIA. Leaving Iconium they came to Lystria in Cilicia where they so captivated the people with their new doctrine that they were taken for gods and the Apostles barely escaped having sacrifices made to them. They strenuously opposed the action of the enthusiasts which evidently incensed the Lystrian priests and Paul was almost stoned to death by them.

12—DERBE. The next day the two preachers left Lystra for Derbe where a large number of converts were made as had been the case in all the places before mentioned.

13—ATTALIA. This ended their first missionary journey and they returned through the towns they had previously visited, ordained elders in every congregation, took ship from Attalia and sailed (14) direct for Antioch (Autumn A.D. 49).

15—JERUSALEM. During the absence of Paul and Barnabas, the Antioch church which was composed mostly of Gentiles, had been disturbed by the Jewish Christians who demanded them to be circumcised before they could become members of the church and the Apostles went to Jerusalem where a council was held and the decision was favorable to the Gentiles. Silas returns with them to Antioch.

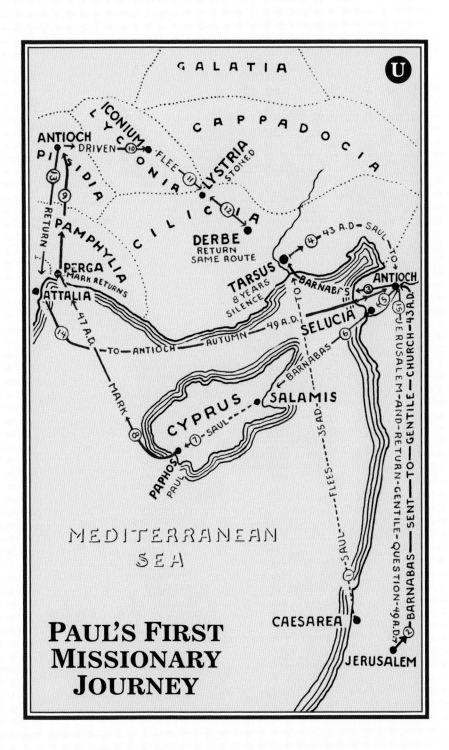

PAUL'S FIRST MISSIONARY JOURNEY

22 PAUL'S SECOND MISSIONARY JOURNEY
AD50 – AD53

Note: Felix procurator.

1—ANTIOCH. Paul leaves Antioch with Silas and starts upon his second missionary tour. The first stop was at Derbe (2) where Paul had been before and they made the trip by land.

ACTS 16

3—LYSTRA. After encouraging the little church, he advanced to Lystra where we are first introduced to Timothy.

6—TROAS. The Trio, including Timothy, now start out depending entirely upon the direction of the Holy Spirit and finally arrive at Troas where the company is probably joined by Luke. Here Paul saw the "Man of Macedonia" in a vision and did not hesitate to go to their aid.

7—SAMOTHRACIA. They sailed from Troas to the little Island of Samothracia the first day and the next they reached the main land at Neapolis (8) at the northermost point of the Aegaean Sea.

9—PHILIPPI. Immediately they went to Philippi, the capital: here Lydia was made a convert and when a certain soothsayer was converted, it resulted in Paul and Silas being cast into prison. Then followed an earthquake which resulted in the conversion of the jailor himself.

ACTS 17

12—THESSALONICA. Paul left Philippi next morning and passed Amphipolis (10) and Apollonia (11) without incident, as Thessalonica seemed to have been his objective.

13—BEREA. After a turbulent campaign in Thessalonica, the little company arrived at Berea where they found a noble community and they made a large number of converts.

14—ATHENS. Paul left Timothy and Silas at Berea and took a few of the Berean brethren and sailed to Athens. Here in this classic city he delivered his most scientific discourse and found a less hostile people than he had heretofore encountered.

ACTS 18

15—CORNITH. From Athens Paul crossed over to Corinth the largest city in Greece, (A.D. 51) where he met Aquila and Priscilla, remained for a year and a half, and wrote the Epistles to the Thessalonians. He supported himself by his trade, tentmaking.

16—CENCHREA. He then determined to return to Jerusalem, so he crossed over to Cenchrea where he "made a vow and shaved his head" and sailed immediately to Ephesus (17) where he left Priscilla and Aquila, promising soon to return.

18—CAESAREA. From Ephesus he sailed direct to Caesarea and presumably went on to Jerusalem (19) but no mention is made of this.

So we next find him at Antioch where he remained a short time and wrote the letter to the Galatians (A.D. 54).

Nero succeeds Claudius at this time.

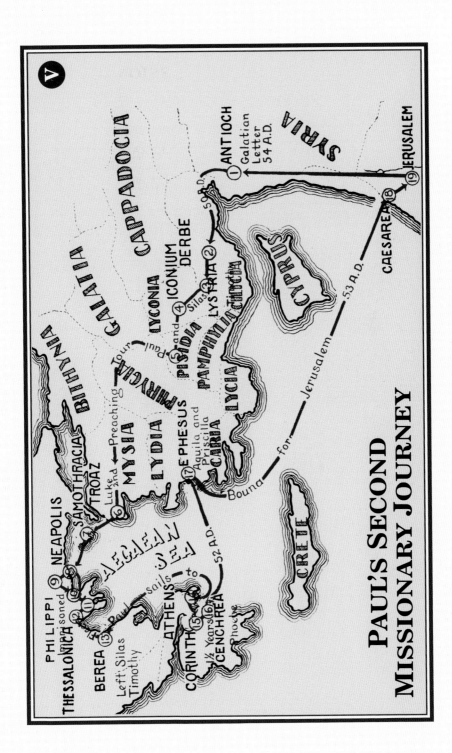

PAUL'S SECOND
MISSIONARY JOURNEY

23 PAUL'S THIRD MISSIONARY JOURNEY
Nero is Emperor – Felix is Procurator
AD54 – AD57

1—ANTIOCH. Upon the Third Missionary Tour, Paul went by land direct to Ephesus (2) where he remained for three years and succeeded in spite of the many odds that were against him. During his stay in Ephesus he wrote the first letter to the Corinthians.

ACTS 20

6—CORINTH. In A.D. 56 Paul left Ephesus and visited his Macedonian churches (3-4-5) during which time he wrote the second letter to the Corinthians and finally he revisited Corinth where he again remained quite some time and wrote his letter to the Romans and sent it to them by Phoebe, a Deaconess of the church at Cenchrea. (16 Map 11) A.D. 57.

Paul is now to return to Jerusalem. He determines to visit the churches he had organized in Macedonia and sent Timothy direct to Troas (8) while he himself made a circuit of the churches (7-4-3) taking offerings for the poor at Jerusalem.

8—TROAS. Finally he arrived at Troas, preached all night, healed Ustychus of a broken neck and from there he walked to Assos (9) where he took ship to Mitylene and the next day to the Island of Chios.

10—MILETUS. At Miletus where he arrived next day the ship tarried for some days and the elders from the Ephesus church met him there and he gave them his last instructions and benediction. They wept and kissed each other and separated never to meet again.

ACTS 21-22

11—PATARA. Loosing from Miletus they spent the next night at Coos, then at Rhodes and the third at Patara. Here Paul and his party changed ships and sailed direct to Tyre.

12—TYRE. It took a week to unload the cargo at Tyre and Paul spent all his time with the little church there.

13—PTOLEMAIS. The next day they were in Ptolemais and he spent a day there with the brethren.

14—CAESAREA. Another day brought them to Caesarea. He tarried with Philip "many days", and his friends pleaded with him not to go to Jerusalem after they had heard the prophesy of Agabus regarding the evil that would befall him there.

15—JERUSALEM. But he was determined, and went to the Holy City in spite of their advice. He was cordially received by the church but soon his enemies had him under arrest and would have taken his life had they not discovered he was a Roman citizen.

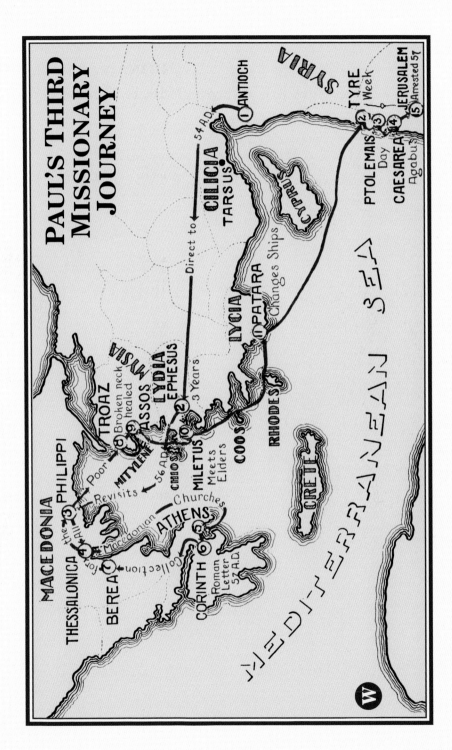

PAUL'S THIRD MISSIONARY JOURNEY

MEDITERRANEAN SEA

24 PAUL TAKEN PRISONER TO ROME
AD58 – AD67

1—JERUSALEM. That night the Lord promised him that he should go to Rome and before morning he was on his way to Caesarea accompanied by nearly 500 soldiers who went as far as Antipatris (2) and from there seventy cavalrymen delivered him to Felix the Procurator at the capital.

3—CAESAREA. Paul was incarcerated at Caesarea for more than two years. (A.D. 57-59). Felix gave him a hearing, he was again heard by Festus the successor of Felix and later by Herod Agrippa, but he had appealed to Rome and there he must go.

ACTS 27

4—SIDON. Paul is now placed in charge of Julius, a Centurion, and accompanied by Luke and Aristarchus, starts for Rome. The ship halted at Sidon and Paul was permitted to go ashore and "refresh himself with his friends." (59 A.D.)

5—MYRA. From Sidon, the ship keeping close to the Cilician shore, landed at Myra in Lycia where they changed boats for the rest of the trip.

6—FAIR HAVENS. The ship started west but it was caught in the high wind and driven south past the east coast of Crete, but made a safe landing at Fair Havens, a port on the south shore.

They left Fair Havens in spite of Paul's advice not to do so and were soon overtaken with another storm called Euroclydon which again drove them south, barely missing the Island of Clauda.

MALTA. The ship was caught in the storm in the open sea and was fairly blown to pieces; the cargo was thrown overboard and for two weeks the sun was not seen. But by following Paul's advice they were enabled to make a safe landing at Malta without the loss of a single life although the ship was shattered to pieces.

ACTS 28

They remained at Malta for three months during which time Paul was bitten by a viper and the natives looked upon him as a god because he suffered no inconvenience from it.

7—SYRACUSE. They were then carried by another ship to Syracuse in Sicily.

8—RHEGIUM. The next stopping place was Rhegium on the Straights of Messina and from thence they sailed to Puteoli (9) a suburb of Naples, where there was already a little church and Paul was permitted to go ashore and tarried with them seven days.

10—APPII FORUM. In the meantime a group of Christians from Rome came to meet Paul and the two parties met at the Forum of Appius.

12—ROME. Then he was met by another group twenty miles out of Rome at Three Taverns (11) and they all marched into the Eternal City together (March A.D. 60) Paul was committed to prison but was afterward allowed many liberties and even "dwelt two whole years in his own hired house and received all that came unto him, preaching the kingdom of God with all confidence, no man forbidding him."

This closes the account of Paul as set down in the Book of Acts, but tradition supplies the following:

61, 62 A.D. Paul writes the Epistles to Philemon, Colossians, Ephesians and Philippians. He was tried early in 62 and acquitted.

63 A.D. Paul Visits Macedonia, Asia Minor, Crete and Spain. He writes to Titus and his first letter to Timothy.

64 A.D. Great persecution of Christians.

66 A.D. Winters at Nicopolis, sent to Rome, second trial and condemned. Second Letter to Timothy. Martyrdom (67 A.D.) Age 68 years, 35 years of Christian service.